PREFACE

Sleep is one of the greatest riddles of our existence. It is an absolute necessity for the refreshment of each one of us, yet natural science can give virtually no explanation of how this is done. And the reason for this is clear – it is not only a natural but primarily also a spiritual process. Understanding therefore depends on the research of the spiritual scientist, and pre-eminently on that of Rudolf Steiner, whose self-development uniquely qualified him for such a task. We are concerned here only with human sleep – although the sleep of animals may superficially look similar, the difference in soul constitution and the lack of an individual ego in the animal means that it is entirely different. In sleep we unfold our cosmic nature – 'the true anthropos'.

This is the first integrated account of the many aspects of sleep which Steiner described in over 330 of his lectures spanning 17 years. His following remarks may set the tone. "We can never encompass reality with one description; we invariably give only one part of the full reality when we describe anything, and need always first to seek light from other sides in turn in order to illuminate in the right way the fraction of reality already given." "It is very necessary to gather together carefully the items of concrete knowledge that have been given, and to correlate them." That is what is attempted here. But "it is one of the most difficult things for ordinary understanding to see that the same words in a different context can mean something different." [1]

The following study is also the first attempt to describe in anthroposophical terms the process of bodily restoration (see sec.20) and relate it to the basic scientific concept of rapid eye movements. Orthodox scientific research describes stages of deepening and lighter sleep, but it does not enlighten us as to the underlying causes of this activity throughout the night. Through Steiner's insight into the soul and spiritual worlds, he describes clearly the three phases passed through in sleep, and the paths into the starry worlds which we ourselves undertake unconsciously every night. He compares the first phase of sleep to thinking in the waking state, the second to feeling and the third phase of deeper sleep as comparable to willing in the waking state. But he also gives many other descriptions without mentioning the phase concerned, and the editors have therefore had to exercise their own judgment in placing these within the whole. We have the impression that in principle he gained experience of the first phase of sleep through Imagination, the second phase through Inspiration, and the third phase through Intuition.* In general much of the earlier stages continues while the deeper stages are added. Even in a nap, we progress rapidly through the different phases.

What follows is all based directly on Rudolf Steiner's words in précis (in some cases on unrevised translations, and in the case of lectures before about 1908 on notes made by participants) *except* that Sections 6 and 20 are largely our own conclusions

---

*Imagination, Inspiration and Intuition are the three stages of higher knowledge – see *Occult Science* (5)

The Wonders of Sleep

The Wonders of Sleep

An Anthroposophical Study

from the works of
Rudolf Steiner

compiled and edited by
Richard Seddon and Dr. Jean Brown

**Wynstones
Press**

Published by
Wynstones Press
Stourbridge
England.

www.wynstonespress.com

First edition 2012

Cover illustration by Veronica Murray.

Printed in England.

ISBN 9780 946206 73 5

Being Awake
In the universal spheres of spirit
Stands erect the spatial form of man.
In the cosmic realms of astral being
Weaves and streams the human force of life.

Sleeping
In the soul's ongoing rounds of freedom
The rule of human instinct is at rest.
In the sun-bright kingdoms of the spirit
There springs to life the human power of thought.

Rudolf Steiner
from 'Wahrspruchworte.'
tr. Pauline Wehrle

CONTENTS

Preface			9
I	**Introduction**		
	1.	Natural Scientific Research	13
	2.	Sleep and the Human being	16
	3.	The Evolution of Sleeping and Waking	20
II	**Going to Sleep**		
	4.	Tiredness – The Need for Sleep	26
	5.	Falling Asleep	31
	6.	Overcoming Sleeplessness	38
	7.	Loss of Consciousness	41
III	**First Phase of Sleep**		
	8.	The Soul and its Environment	45
	9.	Deeper Experiences	50
	10.	Bodily Processes	55
	11.	The Beginnings of Karma	60
IV	**Second Phase of Sleep**		
	12.	Body and Soul	63
	13.	Solar and Planetary Experiences	66
	14.	The Work of the Third Hierarchy	70

V	**Third Phase of Sleep**	
	15. Relating to the Fixed Stars	75
	16. Relating to Physical Processes	80
	17. Morality and Sleep	84
	18. Sleepwalking	89
	19. The Forming of Karma	91

VI	**Reversion to First Phase**	
	20. The Bodily Restorative Processes	95

VII	**Waking Up**	
	21. The Approach	100
	22. Return to the Body	104
	23. Awaking to Outer Life	110
	Verse: Waking from Sleep	114

VIII	**Dreams**	
	24. Introduction	117
	25. In Relation to the Body	121
	26. In Relation to the Outside World	126
	27. In Relation to the Spiritual World	128
	28. Dreams and Destiny	134
	29. Transforming Dream Life	136

References	140

arising from his work. Apparent contradictions and gaps may occasionally be found, where we have not discovered a higher explanation by Steiner that would resolve them. References which seem particularly significant are dated.

We should like to express our special thanks to the Librarians at Rudolf Steiner House, to Veronica Murray for her cover design, and to Stuart Brown for his ever-willing help with the computer work in the preparation of the manuscript.

Richard Seddon
Jean Brown
Christmas 2010

I INTRODUCTION

1. Natural Scientific Research

A convenient survey contained in the online *Encyclopaedia Britannica* 2010 articles entitled 'Sleep' and 'Dreams' may be outlined as follows:

Sleep is a normal, easily reversible, recurrent and spontaneous state of decreased and less efficient responsiveness to external stimulation. There is no single, perfectly reliable criterion of sleep; it is defined by the convergence of observations satisfying several different motor, sensory and physiological criteria. It is a regularly occurring suspension of consciousness that serves recuperative and adaptive functions.

Sleep varies in depth, and in the adult the usual progression from light to deep sleep is in the sequence 1-2-3-4-3-2-1. The four stages of increasing depth are determined by brain patterns of electrical activity as recorded in electroencephalogram tracings. Recorded frequency is 4–7 hertz at stage 1, 12–14 hz at stage 2, but generally only 2–4 hz at stages 3 and 4, though of higher amplitude. Voltage increases from stage 1 to 2, and again to stages 3 and 4. The fourth stage, which is increased after physical exercise or after abnormally extended wakefulness, is only arbitrarily distinguished from the third.

Research distinguishes between the absence or presence of rapid eye movements (REMs) – an average of seventy to ninety minutes without such movements (non-REM sleep),

followed by initially five to fifteen minutes with REMs. The
sequence of the different stages is commonly repeated several
times a night, the periods of deeper sleep being gradually short-
ened and the periods with REMs lengthened, thus:

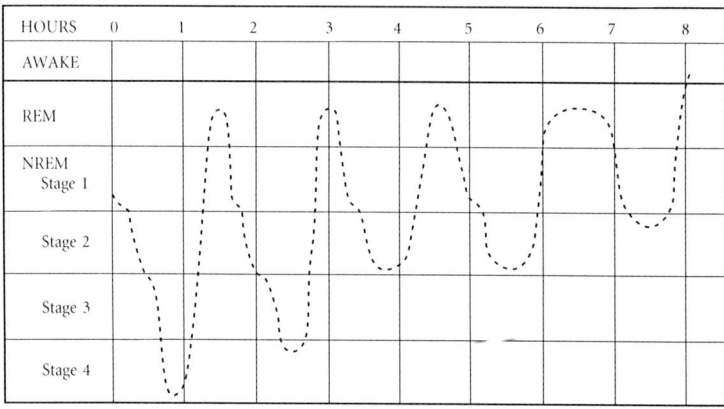

Diagram 1

Normal adult sleep requirement varies from six to nine
hours, with seven and a half hours as average. Body temperature
drops during the early hours of sleep, reaching a low point after
five or six hours, then rises toward the morning awakening. Only
one fifth of the time asleep is spent in REM sleep, which rarely
occurs at onset.

Young infants sleep intermittently for an average of
sixteen hours, half of which may be REM sleep, occurring particularly at sleep onset. It has been suggested that the high
frequency and priority in the night of their REM sleep may
reflect a need for stimulation from within to permit orderly
maturation of the central nervous system. From infancy to early
childhood the sleep pattern gradually shifts to a single uninter-

rupted period. The elderly may revert to napping by day and sleeping only a few hours at night.

During non-REM sleep skeletal muscles are relaxed – mobility decreases as depth of sleep increases. Most functions of the autonomic nervous system, such as pulse and breathing, decrease their rate of activity, and this seemingly restful state appears capable of supporting the recuperative functions (though no indication is given of how this occurs). There is a theory that this type of sleep is a state of 'bodily repair' whilst that with rapid eye movements is one of 'brain repair' (but see sec. 20). Sleepwalking (unexplained) occurs only in deep sleep, whereas sleeptalking occurs in stage 2; neither is associated with dreaming.

When REMs are present, the electroencephalogram patterns are superficially similar to those of wakefulness. It is a state of diffuse bodily activation with a relatively high level of autonomic nervous activity – the brain shows higher oxygen consumption with increased blood flow and temperature; both heart and respiration rates are higher with an increase of blood pressure. However, these periods show a relatively low rate of gross bodily movement, but with some periodic twitching of the muscles of the face and extremities. REM sleep is subjectively felt as deep, perhaps due to vivid dreams. The current tendency is to consider REM sleep as a unique state, sharing properties of both light and deep sleep.

Dreaming, a distinctive phenomenon of sleep, has since the dawn of human history given rise to countless beliefs, fears, and conjectures regarding its perplexing nature. Dreams have been regarded as: life in a special dream-world, events demanding fulfilment, divine messages or prophecies, healing advice (temple sleep), "reduction of sensory function, external or bodily, favouring susceptibility of dreams to emotional subjective distortions"(Aristotle), sources of literary or scientific inspiration, expressions of hopes or fears (psychoanalysis). Among Freud's earliest writings was The Interpretation of Dreams (1899). He insisted that dreams are the royal road to the unconscious. Physiologically, it is thought that the dream state depends on an area within the brain stem, the pontine tegmentum. The discovery that REMs seem often to signal that a person is dreaming, and that vivid dreams are primarily associated with REM sleep, has led to increasing medical research.

Indeed, no single encompassing natural scientific theory is available with regard to the cause and mysterious nature of sleep or dreams.

2. Sleep and the Human Being

Waking and sleeping form a rhythmic polarity experienced by every human being. Anyone who did not repeatedly renew his exhausted forces through sleep would clearly destroy his life. Similarly, a way of thinking not fructified by knowledge of hidden worlds would ultimately lead to emptiness and desolation. It is thus increasingly important that all who give any thought to the meaning of existence on earth should be alive to the significance of what happens in sleep.

It is obvious that while the body lies asleep in bed, the vital functions such as breathing, pulse and digestion, albeit somewhat modified, continue to sustain it. These are processes of the *etheric* body, life body or body of formative forces, without which the physical body on its own would disintegrate in death. It is equally evident that our thoughts, mental images, pains and pleasures, and the power to direct the will are all blotted out; but they reappear on waking, and cannot therefore be annihilated, only withdrawn into another mode. These are carried by the *astral* body or consciousness body, which belongs to an environment of soul and spirit. The etheric body has to be rhythmically endowed with the appropriate forces by the astral body, which in turn during sleep draws the pattern forms or archetypes from the same universe of pure soul and spirit that is the source of the original creative patterns of the human being. While we are awake our soul puts its own patterns drawn from the day's experiences in place of those creative patterns, leading to fatigue; whilst we sleep the astral body acquires newly-strengthened powers of refreshment which it brings back to the body. The problem is – how does this take place?

Sleep can only be understood as an inner rhythm at the basis of soul life. It is by no means just rest, as is often supposed; both ego and astral body are significantly active realities, but we have no organs by which to become conscious of the happenings in which we are involved. Every time we display consciousness, we destroy the sprouting and budding processes of our organism; the more conscious and alert we become, the more do we insert dead elements into our living human being. Whereas it is thinking that disintegrates the nerve substance, it is particularly through our personal interests, the sympathy and antipathy which we bring to external objects, that destruction is brought about more widely. Then sleep has the task of dissolving these dead elements away, except for certain residues which lie at the foundation of memory; were everything to be dissolved by sleep, we should have no memory.

Since the astral body no longer needs during sleep to

transform the outer physical processes into sensations, it can instead produce new forces for the physical and especially for the etheric body. In sleep the astral bodies of all human beings are much alike – the original wisdom still lives in our dormant souls. We are kept separate in sleep only by a strong longing for our physical body; otherwise we should drift through one another all night long. The regular alternation of sleeping and waking builds up the physical body, and enables us to think effectively.

The whole process during sleep is of course normally unconscious, to such an extent that when we look back in memory we join together what we have done by day, and ignore the times spent asleep. On inspection, however, the periods of sleep appear like dark patches in life; and these darknesses are actually *what we call our ego*, for our ego as we can address it on earth is in the first place a darkness of life, an emptiness, a non-existence.[2] To say with Descartes 'I think, therefore I am' ignores sleep, and must imply intervals when the ego ceases to exist.

On the physical plane the ego lives as an act of will. The mental image of the ego arises by day from acts of will striking against the body as a mirror; we thus become aware of ourselves. Sleep consists in suppressing all willing – we cannot will while we are asleep – so that the mental image of the ego is lost. Daytime life is actually a weaker form of life in sleep; we are simply more conscious of it because it continually impinges on the etheric and physical bodies. The more intensive though indefinite activity of sleep life cannot strike on anything, the soul being now withdrawn outside the body, and therefore remains unconscious.

The memory of having slept, and also indefinite recollections of our sleeplike willing, give us a *feeling* for the ego, and it is this feeling, not the mental image of the ego, that depends on these gaps of sleep. As an ego we would feel no connection with the body if we did not leave it during sleep and seek for it again on waking. Through the deprivation undergone we feel united with the body, so that we keep a hold on it until we die; if we lacked this feeling of self we would fail to return from sleep.

Prior to our present ego-being there existed a divine pre-human creature. All that part of it which has been mastered by the ego is each night torn away from the physical and etheric bodies; but the rest remains, firmly implanted there, and watches over these bodies.[3] The truth is that we never bring *our real 'I'* with us from the spiritual world into the physical. What we call 'I' is only a picture, an image of our true human being. In sleep or dream our real 'I', though as yet little developed, is much more active than when we are awake.

Our state of sleep is objectively much more like that between death and rebirth than is usually thought – the difference is that we are then conscious of the world we are in and of what is happening, whereas in sleep we are not. It cannot be denied that the worlds we enter in sleep are real, because they have real effects – we awake with fresh forces. The essential feature of sleep is that we achieve something remarkable, but are unaware of it – if we were to play a conscious part we should ruin everything and harm our development; we are not yet capable of being conscious participants. Of all that the spirit has to achieve on earth through us, by far the greater part is done during sleep. Human evolution depends entirely on this.

We do not only sleep at night: our willing is always asleep. Moreover, with every inhalation of breath we go to sleep a little; on exhaling we wake up. In synthesising we fall asleep, in analysing we wake a little. The satisfaction of ownership puts us to sleep, the necessity of struggling in life wakes us up. Listening is nothing but to 'sleep oneself' into a conversation, comprehension is a kind of waking up. During sleep bridges can be built connecting all human beings. While awake the person who confronts us seeks to put us to sleep in order that a bridge may be built to him; and we do the same to him. Only when asleep do we establish a true and straightforward relationship with another person.

Each time we go to sleep or wake up we pass through a zero point, and this rhythm can only be depicted by a lemniscate. In childhood we wake virtually the same as when we went to sleep, but as we develop we press forward a little in evolution.

To research accurately what happens between falling asleep and waking is one of the most difficult investigations that can be undertaken in spiritual science.[4] The experiences to be described reveal themselves only to Imagination, Inspiration and Intuition, not in the guise of memory but as if in a psychic review. The spiritual investigator does no more than watch events that happen in sleep to everyone. Once described, however, they can be widely understood.

3. The Evolution of Sleeping and Waking
The sleep condition was once the permanent state of all humanity on the ancient Sun* – plants still have this state of consciousness. Alternation of sleeping and waking was only prepared during the ancient Moon evolution, when the moon already moved around the sun. Sleep was then an exit and

---

* Ancient Sun, ancient Moon, Lemuria and Atlantis are previous stages of earth evolution – see *Occult Science* (4).

entrance of astral and etheric bodies from the physical, for there was no human ego. Separation brought primeval man a clear spiritual picture-consciousness, reunion a darkening – the reverse of the present.

At a very early stage of Earth evolution, before the ego was present, the astral body withdrew with only part of the etheric. Then after the separation of the moon in Lemuria, and after the Fall, an alternation of day and night was brought about. We read in Genesis 2.21: 'The Lord God caused a deep sleep to fall upon the human creature, and he slept'; this is the first alternation of sleeping and waking, prior to which humanity continually perceived spiritual entities. Until the physical body had developed to above the hips, perception of an astral-etheric nature was by means of the pineal gland. Now the eyes were open, and while awake people saw objects darkly, as though wrapped in mist and surrounded by an aura of light; asleep they were conscious of spiritual beings. When at full moon Lemurians slept and the astral body floated above in the moonlight, streams of force passed into the physical body to remove fatigue, restore energy and nourish it.

At first the astral body and ego were within the physical for a very brief portion of the day, but ever shorter grew the night. Into the increasingly dim clairvoyance dispensing Spirits of Love, the Elohim, sent down by night the first streams of natural love; in the moonlight human beings received too, reflected from Jehovah, the forces of matured wisdom; this prepared them to receive later the more spiritualised form of love.[5]

By night the ego and astral body were then entirely within the domain of the Angels, Archangels, Archai and Spirits of Form; whereas the body was within that of the Spirits of Form, Movement, Wisdom and the Thrones. In this way harmful influences brought about by day through the aberrations of the astral body could be made good. Human beings felt immortal, and safe at night in the keeping of the gods. Our dreaming today is a last stunted remnant of their nightly clairvoyance – except that images of colour and form had then a very real meaning, signifying something psychic or spiritual in their environment, for example something harmful to avoid.

During Atlantis nightly clairvoyance became ever dimmer, but people knew the gods as well as they knew beings of flesh and blood. They felt themselves in the sphere where Sun-beings dwell. Their experiences lived on in myths and legends. They still beheld the dazzling astral light, and their deeds were much more automatic than ours. The objects of the outer world were blurred and indistinct, surrounded by auras indicating the presence of spiritual beings. The Atlanteans could perceive the earthly effects of the harmony of the spheres streaming from the sun, and the life pulsating in living beings. By the time of the great shifting of the tectonic plates that brought about the end of Atlantis, objects appeared by day in clearer outlines; but most people had lost at night the gift to look into spiritland, although remnants of clairvoyance continued among the more backward.

The sharp distinction between the unconsciousness of night and day-waking consciousness appeared gradually only after the flood. At first we find conditions like our sleep, but permeated with a consciousness of a world of light-air, of cosmic harmony, and of the battle between good and evil beings. Waking consciousness was dream-like; direct intercourse with spiritual beings lived on in awareness of tree spirits, nymphs of the springs and the like. And men found by day the thoughts inspired by the gods at night. During sleep people were aware of their karma, and indeed far more conscious of it than can be the case today. What we today call waking, an initiate of the Mysteries would then have called sleep, because we are asleep to the spiritual being within our body.

By the Chaldean (third Post-Atlantean) age, objects were still blurred by day, and a spiritual essence rayed from them like spray; whereas in sleep, people were yet aware in mighty ever-changing images of the flux and movement of the life of worlds, they were immersed in the reality of being. Thus the transition was less brusque than today.

The teachers of the Mysteries awakened and clothed in ideas what their pupils now went through unconsciously in sleep, saying: every night you enter spiritually into the midst of all that you perceive with your senses by day – every nightingale, every flower, every stream. Then the pupil could be convinced that the gods whom he experienced in waking dream were also outside in nature.[6]

Three or four thousand years ago, as people were entering sleep, a picture of the Guardian of the Threshold* arose like a dream in their souls, and as they were returning this picture again appeared. Progress in evolution required that we gain freedom by losing spiritual vision, and we had to forfeit also this dream of the Guardian. At the time of the Druids there were three states of consciousness: a dream-like everyday life, a dreamless sleep and a feeling as if gravity had enclosed them in the embrace of the earth. They experienced the phenomena of nature as a living, weaving and surging of spiritual beings.

* See *Occult Science* (5) or p43.

All their thinking was more dream-like, vivid, alive and full of substance than ours, affording a sort of nourishment for the soul as an after-taste of sleep.

From Greece and Rome until the Middle Ages, dreams were still used to enter the spiritual world; blurred images entered sensory perception and pointed to the future. People found it relatively easy to perceive spiritual elements, and to approach spirits and the dead; everywhere colour and sound sparkled with spiritual qualities; waking dreams were realities in the elemental, objective world.

As late as the eighth century, people on waking still had many pictures of their past earthly life. The night was filled with all manner of sounds, a language of spiritual Beings in the light-filled spaces of the cosmos. In this they felt that both good and evil spirits were speaking as they slept. By the eleventh century people still approached sleep in an elemental mood of prayer, full of nature force, experiencing spiritual-etheric auras around the whole of nature, and strove to give themselves over to divine-spiritual powers performing deeds within them. Later than the fifteenth century the spirit was mere tradition, until in the nine-teenth century it was altogether lost. We have only been able on waking to plunge entirely into the physical and etheric bodies since the fifteenth century, and even so not until we reach our 27th or 28th year; conditions will change further with time.

At the present stage of evolution, the Angels are working through the images they create in man's astral body, images that are to configure us for the future, to be achieved by the spiritual soul. But since human beings are refusing to turn to spiritual life at this time of the new millenium, the Angels instead have to try to achieve their aims during sleep by means of the etheric and physical bodies. Here lies great danger. Instead of a deeper interest in every human individual, pernicious instincts connected with sexual life will prevent men from unfolding brotherhood in any form whatever, becoming instead half devils.* True Christianity with complete freedom in religious matters will not be possible for them. Instinctive insight into the medicinal properties of certain substances and treatments will bring about illness for egotistical purposes. And knowledge of certain tremendous mechanical forces will lead technology into desolate waters, of benefit only to human egoism.[7]

Whereas the whole purpose of earlier times was to allow man to enter the spiritual world during sleep, present-day man has to enter the spiritual world in waking consciousness. The very meaning of evolution lies in this – that sleep shall lose its significance for cognition more and more.

---

* Note already the growth of addictive pornography.

II GOING TO SLEEP

4. Tiredness – The Need for Sleep

To say that tiredness causes sleep, as do scientists, is quite different from saying that sleep drives away tiredness. It is not the tiredness, it is the soul's desire to get rid of the tiredness that causes sleep – it is to be regarded as a soul-spiritual phenomenon. We want to sleep, and consequently we feel tired. We sleep because our soul needs the recurrent meeting with the spiritual world. Waking life is no more the cause of sleep than day is the cause of night.

When asleep we experience the body more deeply than when awake, so sleep is in a sense self-enjoyment. It is simply a necessity that we return to the consciousness which we share with the plants – outwardly deep sleep, but inwardly aware of influences throughout the solar system.

In *mental* work our body is excessively active; we cannot normally work with the spirit and soul unless we work inwardly with our body; a dying of organic matter always accompanies mental work such as thinking or reading. With non-stop academic activity there is thus an excessive breakdown of organic matter, which disturbs peaceful sleep.

If the physical brain is tired out, this fatigue is markedly felt in the corresponding etheric part and we notice a blockage. Materialistic thinking does not directly cause the organs of the etheric body to become tired, but the etheric body notices the exhaustion of the physical brain and says: now you must stop, or you will be ill. The physical body falls asleep, but the etheric body becomes restless, drawing the spirit and soul back into it. When we twist and turn in bed healthy life forces are present but the inner being of the life of soul is not engaged, so there is no desire for what would make us truly tired. This must gradually develop into insomnia and the inability to take in any moral or spiritual impulses at all.

The wonderful feelings of reverence for knowledge, which permeated life in the Middle Ages with real re-creative forces for the soul, have to a great extent been lost. With the rise of a more materialistic science stored in libraries and studied with indifference, there is no longer any possibility of getting tired from spiritual knowledge acquired with much effort.[8]

We should be able to carry tiredness within us as a response to ordinary phenomena meeting us in life. Mental images which require effort tire us and help us to sleep, so long as they do not irritate or worry us. They live in that part of the etheric body which belongs to the astral world (sentient body or soul body*), and lead us into that world.

If we have to learn something by heart, it is much better to 'sleep on it'. This applies to other soul activities as well. We can easily convince ourselves that were it not for sleep we could not learn anything for which the soul's contribution is necessary. The natural conclusion is that our soul needs to draw strength from outside the body to replace forces used up whilst within it, so that we bring back strength to develop capacities we could not develop in the body.

* The finer part of the etheric body forming a unity with the sentient soul and shaping the sense organs.

Teachers working out of a real art of education have to consider where the real sources of tiredness lie. Exhaustion in *childhood* may arise from the head region, where the forces working downwards deposit fine salt-like residues throughout the body, affecting the breathing and blood circulation – this brings about an arrhythmic relationship with the outer world. But exhaustion may also arise from the activities of the limbs or the metabolism, where the influence of forces released by heat interferes with the inner rhythm. Tiredness can never originate from the rhythmic middle system itself, from the breathing or blood circulation, which strongly retains a state of equilibrium, obeying its own laws.[9]

Healthy young infants sleep almost continuously. As long as we are growing, the forces that support our growth maintain our brain in a physiologically active condition. As soon as the child begins to think, the brain cells tend towards a death-like condition; the activating forces find it more difficult to reach the brain even during sleep, and it begins to age. But we must still sleep to allow the brain to be reconstituted, rejuvenated by soul-spiritual forces.

Mental work is thus a bodily function, but *physical* work is spiritual. Excessive physical work means that the world spirit that approaches us from outside gains too much power, so that we must give ourselves over to the spirit for too long; we sleep too long. Excessive sleep in turn excites life too strongly, we get a fever and our blood becomes overheated. The important thing is purposeful activity according to the demands not of the body but of our surroundings, or where purposeful movements follow the spirit as a goal, as in eurythmy. In such activities we draw the spirit in and work consciously with it.[10] Muscles and nerves grow tired through conscious activity, but when they serve exclusively organic activity they cannot grow tired.

To sleep unnecessarily does not drive away fatigue, but leads to neurasthenia, where there is imbalance between the processes of the upper and lower poles of the body as a result of over-taxing of the 'organic-intellectual' forces.[11] Excessive sleep can predispose to epidemic illnesses – waking life should not be interrupted by such long periods of sleep. However, the lethargic who like to sleep too long are not in fact inactive, they continually fidget, but without any goal or purpose. If we were able to keep on sleeping, never awaking, we might still have an ego, but could not be conscious of it, because ego-consciousness pre-supposes the employment of senses and brain as instruments. The plant element in our bodies would pass over to the plant rhythm of the year, and instead of daily waking, death would ensue. To take up spiritual scientific truths without falling asleep is a truly effective means of overcoming the habit of sleeping too long!

Lack of sleep causes havoc in our ideas, and to some extent lays waste the soul; we might expect those who suffer from sleeplessness to go to pieces, because of the alternating cycles of build-up and breakdown; but they do not, because most people have so much inherited strength. We realise our need for sleep as a creative element, behind which stands the working of the real 'I'. By knowing that lack of sleep is an obstacle to the ripening of our inner life, we become aware of this real 'I' working within us, not as image but as ceaseless inner force.[12]

The astral forces may work so strongly that we should never leave the physical body at all, were it not so tired by daily life that we need to call on the refreshing powers of sleep. People who say they never sleep have such lively dreams that they feel they have been awake. They easily deceive themselves, they are either often awake or sleep irregularly. If we had to be always awake, we should at least by the time we were twenty become automata, unable to act fully consciously, and look repulsively old, for the forces we need to work inwardly on our organism act only during sleep. The period for which many people say they have not slept is so great that they would have been dead long ago if it were true!

If sleeplessness is due not to physiological causes but to the operation of the will, it is a sign that much will be uplifting in a future life, for the vivifying spiritual element contained in the ego penetrates into life as compensation. To lie in complete restfulness without sleeping, when done of set purpose, brings awareness of the eternal. Sleeplessness can sometimes be a good comforter, and if it were not karmically beneficial in its spiritual aspect it would be much more harmful than it actually is.

Every change which alters in either direction the normal proportion of oxygen to nitrogen in the external atmosphere is associated with disturbances of sleep. The link between ego/astral body and etheric/physical body is a true mirror image of the mixture of these gases in the air, the ratio being approximately 1:4 (21% oxygen, 78% nitrogen). Depending on one's respiratory system and one's relation to the environment, sleeping with an open window may be very healthy for one person, but for another it might be better to air the room first. Healthy instincts must be developed to obtain the proper requirements for sleep. We cannot dictate that people must have seven hours sleep – some who do not need it should have much less, and so on; these matters have a tremendous effect on social life.

5. Falling Asleep

To observe the moment of falling asleep, we have to continue the waking state right into sleep. Only through exercises that render thought as objective as a sense perception can this moment be rightly perceived and grasped. Imagination experiences that we slip out of our body with our independent soul-life and leave our web of thoughts behind. Through self discipline of the will, we can observe going to sleep as something similar to forgetting. What brings about withdrawal from the sense world and entry into supersensible reality is the transformation of the will (a resolution of will whilst awake is a weaker form of this).

When the narrowness of the senses becomes oppressive the soul, wrapped around by sleep, returns itself to itself, fleeing to the spirit's distances. The senses grow dull, as though we were enclosed in a fog which seems cold or offers other feelings at certain points, such as on hands, joints, spine etc. As lethargy overcomes our limbs, our speech, our impressions of taste, smell and hearing, we are drawn out of the body by the power of Mars acting on the sentient soul,* which was aware of the tiredness. This alone would lead to absolutely peaceful, undisturbed sleep. The astral body actually goes out through the whole sense system, although it looks to us as though it passes out only through the head.

We can clearly feel how the ego, which at this stage is rather more extensive than the astral, is at first overwhelmed by images and ideas; these gradually grow dimmer, assuming an independent life like separate clouds at the horizon of consciousness, in which the ego becomes lost. We no longer think in rigid concepts, but solely in pictures, which dissolve contours and

* Experiences related to the senses and emotions – see *Occult Science* (2)

allow everything to interweave and become blurred. We may feel that we somehow drag the whole day's experiences along with us, that they become more and more nebulous, and that we then abandon them; the ailing may even notice a slight feeling of pleasure. The Luciferic* element carries us, quite properly, from waking to sleeping. This leads at length to the experience of Lucifer's true form of sublime beauty as Night Spirit.

We can emancipate ourselves from the temporal alteration of day and night, but not from spatial positioning. In sleep we have to bring our spine into the horizontal like the animal (except perhaps in certain illnesses). During the day the transformation of substance, which takes place through deliberate movements, is both an external process, for which the skin is no barrier, and an internal metabolic process that tires us even when doing nothing. But in sleep, an involuntary transformation of substance belonging to the whole cosmos takes place inside us, for which our skin is the effective barrier. For this we have to escape from the line connecting earth and sun, and must lie down; here, the transformed substance supplies the head. This is of real significance.[13]

When we cannot fall asleep it is good to take up a difficult book or something which requires concentrated thinking – study a mathematical book, for instance – but not a novel that captivates our interest by arousing our emotions; that will only hinder us from going to sleep. Strong emotions, even if joyful, but especially if connected with strong interests or expectations

---

* 'Lucifer' means light-bearer. He is the source of understanding, enthusiasm, beauty and art. But he is also the serpent (Genesis 8), the tempter, who leads us to egoism and vanity. He works within the personality as abstract authority, holding to the past.

of the ego, cause difficulty in going to sleep; they are connected to lower spiritland. But when we accompany mental work with interest and warmth of feeling, this fosters blood activity and the enlivening of matter, which facilitates sleep.

Going to sleep means that we are unconsciously putting a question to the world of spirit: how does my moral constitution appear to the entities in the world of spirit? And on waking up the answer will be different if we moderated any anger the night before, or reduced any offence we felt – an angry mood is as if a stream of volcanic fire were to pour into the world of spirit, and the soul world then has to mitigate this.[14]

When we sleep and thought is inactive, the will is awake and very active, although we cannot observe this. The health or unhealthiness of our will works at night upon our whole condition of life, right into the physical body. Very much depends upon whether we develop a mood of serenity by day, accepting destiny, and thus develop a pleasant warmth, a feeling of well-being. Unhealthiness of will – be it as anger, as apathy and lack of interest, or especially as obstinacy – streams into the body during sleep, causing numerous illnesses which may appear only after years or decades. Good will impulses are intimately connected with a strengthening of the life forces within us.

Nothing refreshes so much as good moral impulses. To observe moral impulses, however, when contours become vague and we can no longer move the limbs, requires great attention. We can experience a kind of waking up, as if our conscience expands, as if the morality of the soul awakens. We may feel bliss at all we have done well, and sense the thought: would that this moment might last for ever (or perhaps a feeling of being torn asunder, if the soul has something for which to reproach itself).

But there is a jolt, an inner movement – a demand the soul makes of itself to pour itself out still more. Then it is lost in the moral life of its environment. This is observable and accessible to everyone, but cannot remain in awareness. Though good spirits protect us from bad spirits appearing, bad deeds hinder sleep even more than emotions; and pangs of conscience make sleep extraordinarily difficult. Such moral aspects of will are connected to higher spiritland.

If we carry over into sleep thoughts of arrogance, vanity or pride, we bring impurity into divine spheres. Or if we have gone to bed in a mood of remorse, we sense this next day in our body as weakness, lethargy, numbness; joy we sense as strength and elevation of spirits. Seeing a eurythmy performance strengthens the soul by bringing it at night into living contact with the supersensible; but if we have too much of it, the soul has a restless night in the spiritual world when we should be properly asleep – the counterpart of physical nervousness. We should go to sleep with thoughts of awe and thankfulness towards the great divine beings, for we could not live one moment longer whilst outside the body were it not for them.

It is wonderful to see how children, until corroded by materialism, enter sleep as if on the wings of their angel, and how they are united with them. Before the change of teeth, the child cannot send into sleep with the same strength as later the force which still has to work with the bodily organisation; it can only send less contoured concepts, yet these can envelop soul-spiritual reality in a better way than sharply outlined mental images. Thus children cannot as yet carry the day's waking experiences into sleep, but instead they settle into the general world order. We must help them to take what we do with them into sleep, then it can flow back from the spiritual world as strength to enable them to become true human beings in physical existence. The feeling-willing being which abandons the body of a younger person during sleep is filled with a reflective-thought element; whereas an older person takes more the forces of character, forces contained more in the developed impulses of the will.

Everyone also poses countless questions and gives information to their beloved dead at the moment of falling asleep. Concepts arising from a special interest which united us during life, or moments when we grew warm at their side in a community which led to common action, are well suited to pass over – we may do this at any time of day, and it will stream over when we fall asleep. Those who have died perceive a tremendous difference between people who are filled only with materialistic feelings and ideas and also take them into sleep, and others who are wholly filled with spiritual ideas and continue to be filled with them during sleep. They are as different as a barren region where people starve and a fruitful area that offers nourishment in abundance.

Unhealthy sleep is one of the most deep-seated causes of illness, especially in relation to certain inner bodily functions. An ego and astral body fed on materialistic ideas alone call forth Ahrimanic* forces which become cultivators of bacilli. These forces work on the internal physical organs.

The best remedy is to fall asleep with spiritual thoughts. But this must become a factor in the community for it may be

---

* 'Ahriman' is Satan, prince of darkness, matter and materialism. He is the source of fear, hatred, lies and deception. He works from outside through the senses and cold intellect, especially in concepts of chance, nationalism and atomism.

of no advantage to the individual if all those around breed bacilli by their materialistic thinking. If we have to fall asleep with pictures of the sick, ourselves filled with selfish fear, injurious forces may enter. However, the effects of a noble disposition and of loving help destroy the imaginations of fear, which are really the fostering forces of our Ahrimanic enemies; such effects could even put an end to epidemics, but this cannot yet be. A great deal depends on the kind of spiritual life we take into sleep; by it we mould our souls into good or bad instruments for sending spiritual forces into those organs which function physically and chemically beneath the threshold of consciousness.[15]

We should develop the meditative mood, even if only by means of the retrospect, creating pictures to take over into the spiritual world. In letting the day pass before us backwards in pictures we create an extract which we take over with us. It must be in reverse, because everything happens like this in the spiritual world. We thus create a transition, so that we can enter more easily. Thinking concentrated by spiritual exercises brings fatigue and drowsiness. If we fall asleep during the retrospect and later remember back, we often find that the meditation has gone further. This may indicate a widening of consciousness.

If people do not deepen themselves spiritually they will not be able to sleep properly. That is the essential thing. And if people undergo no such deepening, then hardly will 1940/1950 have come, and over greater and greater areas, there will be widespread epidemics of sleeplessness;* such people will no longer be able to work for civilisation.[16]

* Insomnia has continued to increase since the 1950s.

During the night, meditations and other exercises reverberate and become constructive forces for the astral body, influencing its work upon the physical and etheric bodies; this makes it possible for good beings to be active. Healthy tiredness should not prevent us from carrying through our concentration exercises and meditation with great exertion of will. On the contrary, nature then takes part of the task from us, since it blunts the outer sense-organs and reduces the sensitivity to the sense world. Precisely when we are tired can we enlighten and warm through our being with the light-filled thoughts of meditation.

Few people sense the harm they inflict on themselves through having entirely laid aside the activity of prayer on going to sleep and awakening. Through evening prayer we take into the spiritual world the forces collected by day. Primitive peoples strengthened their soul through prayer before entering the spiritual world, and drew soul forces from that world after leaving it. If we do not relate to these forces, we do not receive them. However learned the materialist, when he goes to sleep unprepared he stands well below such primitive people; he kills something of the spiritual forces on the physical plane. An hour later he would not recognise himself, but would feel himself spread out over endless space. The Druids ensured that the pupil had twelve helpers to support his ego at this moment but that is no longer possible. The Rosicrucian school instead gave meditations. Today people anaesthetise the pain, but it returns in later incarnations as soul torment. Each esoteric pupil has resolved, albeit unconsciously, to help this suffering of mankind.[17]

People should at least become able gradually to develop the feeling: until I wake my soul will be in the spiritual world. There it will meet with the guiding power of my earth life, which lives in that world and soars around my head. My soul will have the meeting with my genius; the wings of my genius will come in contact with my soul.

6. Overcoming Sleeplessness

In order to obtain benefit from the healing forces we receive during the night, it is essential to be able to enjoy healthy sleep. A good night's sleep changes our whole outlook on the world and allows us to participate in our daily tasks with inner strength and positivity.

The underlying causes of restless nights and poor sleeping habits have to be carefully and *individually* considered. Innumerable physical and soul ailments – serious and trivial – may give rise to troublesome sleep patterns. In the child, over-stimulation before bedtime, anxieties, irregular meal-times or lack of daily rhythms all tend towards disturbed nights. Similarly, the adult may feel over-loaded with the day's problems and family worries, or perhaps has been over-indulging in television, with little possibility of being swept over into the oblivion of the night. Knowing that "lack of sleep creates havoc in our ideas and to some extent lays waste the soul"(p29), is a worthy incentive to search for the underlying cause.

Erratic sleep patterns in the very young and in the elderly can cause considerable distress. The newly-born have to adapt to new ways of breathing, of feeding and of sleeping; and it may take many months before healthy patterns of sleep can arise. Such problems are more common in first-born babies due to the over-worrying, insecure mother. In such cases, wise counselling from grandmother, health visitor etc. can rapidly bring about improvement. In the elderly, an opposite shift can become apparent – with less extensive periods of nocturnal sleep and a return to the intermittent sleep pattern of early childhood. Cat-napping becomes common throughout the day and may be difficult to overcome. "In sleep, the soul enjoys its own bodily nature. The pensioner can overdo this and sleep when not at all tired!"[18]

However, the body out of its own individual requirement of sleep may refuse entry to the spirit for just as long as is necessary, without the need of artificially induced sleep.[19]

Recommendations have been made in Section 5 to aid the overcoming of insomnia, but there are further remedies which can be considered without resorting to the allopathic 'sleeping pill'. One's nightly pre-bedtime routine may need to be changed. A herbal tea such as malva compositum (blue mallow and lavender flowers with valerian root BP), followed by a warm lavender bath or a hot footbath prior to bed-time, may prove beneficial, so too copper ointment gently massaged over the abdomen.

A strong endeavour to focus on the day's happenings in reverse will, for many, aid in crossing the threshold (p43), whereas for others, medicinal remedies can be introduced to enhance the ability to sleep, e.g. phosphorus given in the appropriate potency drives the astral body and ego out of the body and sulphur activity has this capacity to a lesser extent. The resources from the mineral and plant worlds are manifold. Avena sativa compositum, zinc valerian or argentum (silver) preparations* can be considered; argentum per bryophyllum (a vegetabilised silver preparation) is particularly helpful for one with an hysteric

* Argentum D6 helps during the waxing moon, when silver forces are directed to the metabolic pole, and phosphorus D6 during the waning moon.

constitution. These are not strong soporifics, but aid in calming the over-active astral forces, leading us into peaceful sleep.

If the astral body and the ego, in a person who has developed an abnormality in his constitution, become during sleep too strongly rooted in the world outside, and take up too much of the cosmic spirituality, their effects on the body become over strong, causing undue hardening. An older person may try to resist this through insomnia; an appropriate lead preparation will ward off the sclerosis.[20]

Depending on the cause of the insomnia specific eurythmy exercises are recommended to encourage the onset of sleep, for which consultation with a trained eurythmy therapist is necessary. For example, 'veneration A (ah)', carried out regularly prior to bed-time, is advocated in those cases where the day's impressions and thoughts about the day's events are a hindrance to sleep. A further powerful exercise – the word 'hallelujah'– gives strength to the etheric and leads the soul out into the planetary spheres. To do this exercise correctly requires considerable practice.[21]

Much advice regarding sleeping problems in children can be found in *A Guide to Child Health* by Michaela Glockner and Wolfgang Goebel.[22] Further guidance can be sought from the anthroposophical pharmacists, Weleda UK Ltd, Heanor Road, Ilkeston, DE7 8DR. If insomnia persists, consultation with a doctor is advisable. (J.B.)

7. Loss of Consciousness

It is only what proceeds from the head organisation, the senses and nerves, that is dimmed or darkened in sleep. We are not conscious during sleep because no destructive process, the basis of consciousness, is at work; the force which creates consciousness is instead used constructively. Sleep extinguishes ordinary consciousness because it carries us out into the germinating life of earth as it springs forth into the living macrocosm. By day we lift ourselves with our own ego-being out of the being of the world in order to attain free self-consciousness, but in sleep we re-unite with it.

Even by day the ego and astral parts of the head cannot unite completely with the physical and etheric parts; they continue to experience a life of their own outside it. Thinking depends on their activity outside being reflected by the physical-etheric of the head, providing the images for everyday consciousness. For waking consciousness our brain cells must be completely at rest, enabling us to think. To lose consciousness in fainting or in sleep means that our life forces overwhelm the forces of waking consciousness; the brain cells, which are constantly in the process of dying, begin to receive a fraction more life and will-force from the body. They summon up the will to move (which they cannot do) and become restless, so the mirror is blurred. As a result of this inner restlessness of the brain, we begin to lose consciousness.

The truth is that when awake we extend with our ego and astral body over that part of the world which we survey, whilst the eye in unison with the brain reflects back to the soul that with which it is living. But take away the mirror, which happens in sleep, and the reflection is no longer there.

To see the spiritual facts around us during sleep at this present stage would actually be highly dangerous, because the astral body would flow out in all directions, while the ego would become dissolved. We should thus be able to envisage pictures of the spiritual world in our astral body, but not understand them, because that requires the forces of insight and discernment which only the ego can bring. We should become frenzied, torn hither and thither, swimming without individuality or direction in a sea of astral events. Therefore the ego, because it is not yet sufficiently developed nor strong enough, reacts upon the astral body and prevents it from consciously entering the spiritual which is its true home.[23] Thus in sleep we are fortunate to withdraw the understanding from the physical brain, and then have that of the supersensible world. We do not yet want to develop our consciousness to bring this cognition into our sense organisation, as we must do in the future; during sleep we are becoming more refined, more spiritual.

The will element – that is, the ego – relates to the entities of the spiritual world during sleep in a way that is much more real than the maya-like way our physical body relates to its environment by day. The parts of our being which remain in a continual state of sleep – such as the heart activity, the digestive process, in fact all our inner physical processes – continue throughout life under the influence of the super-physical. Hence, to find the working of the extra-earthly we must penetrate to what is enclosed within our skin.

When all consciousness is obliterated we are naturally too little aware, too much engrossed in our own evolution. Here (in sleep) Lucifer has the upper hand in our astral body. The ideas called forth by Ahriman in day consciousness, which he causes to harden and crystallise, are dissolved and made to disappear by Lucifer. Everything becomes picture; only when we dream are Lucifer and Ahriman in equilibrium.

During sleep we are protected by the Guardian of the Threshold from becoming conscious of the surrounding spiritual world. Otherwise we would experience a kind of burning up, a kind of extinguishing of the human being – a world of burning, consuming fire, engulfing everything presented by the sense world, a world of thoroughly destructive forces.[24] Instead of perceiving objective spiritual reality we would perceive only the effects of the grotesque, fantastic images and forms not belonging to our humanity that we ourselves take with us into the spiritual world – the worst that is in us, everything not in keeping with the truth. It is always a sign that what we see are fantasies if animal forms appear. Fortunately, we stand unconsciously before the Guardian of the Threshold every night. We confront ourselves, which is the same thing as standing before the Guardian, for as long as our sleep lasts. He shows us what is lacking in us when we try to enter into the macrocosm, and what we must make of ourselves in order to be able, little by little, to grow into that world. The Guardian denies us direct entry to the spiritual world until we are ready for it. To enter safely we need only develop greater and greater inner strength.

The question of consciousness is all-important. We need to develop a feeling for its different states, nuances such as drowsiness or agitation, and awareness of how much or how little attention to pay to them. We must relate such differences to everything we do. The presence of a sense for the rightness of things in varying situations is only another state of consciousness. Spiritual science itself may be met with a good deal of sleepiness!

Dazed states or loss of consciousness are similar but not identical to sleep; the constitution is left floating between sleeping and waking. Astral body and ego may for example withdraw only partially from the sense-nerve system; then the head tends towards sleep but the metabolic-limb and rhythmic systems do not, hence the head is dazed or dulled while the rest of the body functions as when normally awake. This condition also results from ingesting lead or a lead compound. Lead forces out the astral body and ego, causing healthy people to faint or succumb to dizziness. It also hinders the astral body and ego from acting on us from outside, preventing their centripetal effects, so that we fall asleep incompletely.

The arising of dreams will be considered in later sections.

III FIRST PHASE OF SLEEP

8. The Soul and its Environment

We have seen that the astral body leaves the body during sleep, but this is mainly from the head; the lower part is in fact more closely connected with the lower part of the body than by day, although a portion of it passes out below.

On falling asleep the *ego* very quickly envelops the astral body; and because it confronts the world without any support it is unable to perceive anything, so we slip into unconscious sleep. The everyday ego must be given up, because it cannot live beyond the sphere of the outer sense world. Thus every time we go to sleep the egoity is dimmed, for beyond the tapestry of the senses lies the world where, to begin with, the I-power, as it develops for human existence, has no place at all.

The upper ego aura, separated from the lower part at the throat, is directed upwards and outwards from the head as rays; it shines and sparkles, soon becomes vague, and vanishes entirely to one side into the warmth of the outer world. The lower ego aura, meanwhile, is more closely united with the body than by day, denser and more compact. Turned downwards, larger, and darkly tinged with threads of deep red, it becomes opaque as it spreads out below as rays into the indefinite, and is particularly exposed to the influence of Ahriman (Diagram 2).

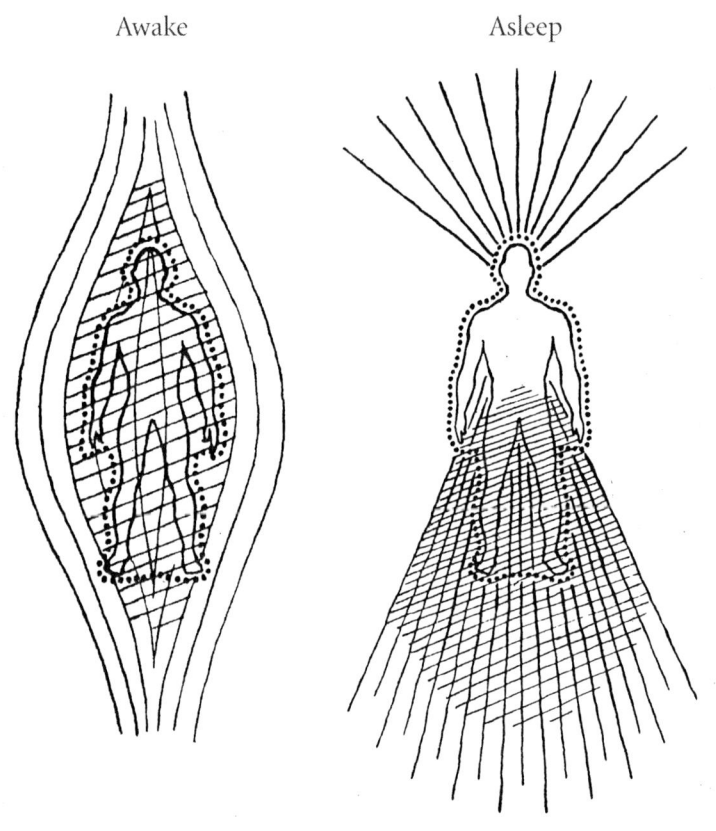

Diagram 2

The *astral* aura of the head rises into the astral world, where it forms something like a spiral mist consisting of many streams and sparkles of light. The lower part of the astral aura (which is not separated) is, on the other hand, more exposed to Lucifer, its indefinite continuation below the diaphragm becoming darker and darker.[25] It is as if two intertwining spirals or '6-figures' were to form, but as both the upward extension and that which is continuous with the body are soon invisible, the phenomenon takes on an egg-shape. The after-effects of what we experienced by day remain in the astral body, except that our thoughts do not remain in the form in which we harboured them, nor as words; remnants, vestiges still adhere, but nothing more.

Our astral body – virtually recent memories, swirling in and through one another in a kind of eddy – then unites in sleep with the spiritual forces behind nature. It is then spread out in the environment and moves on waves of air, but is not far away. Memories connect with the active forces within the minerals and plants, behind the clouds and so on. Experiences widely separated in time and space are now in juxtaposition, and parts of the content are eliminated, so that the whole life of memory is transformed. The inner spiritual core of nature harbours especially the soul elements of childhood. People love the rose because – although they do not know this – roses take in our very first childhood memories while we sleep.[26]

If we had no memories, sleep could not help us at all. This is very important. It is only because we preserve in subconscious memory what we experience during sleep, even though we know nothing of it, that we are not given over entirely to a materialistic way of thinking. If we have any sort of spiritual ideas during the day, we owe it to our memory. For today, as earth-bound man, we only come into touch with the spirit during sleep.[27]

Both ego and astral body live now in the world of the three elemental kingdoms, described in the book *Theosophy* (III,5), which indwell the other three outwardly manifest kingdoms of nature. This is a world of beings with no actual physical body and yet not of a purely supersensible nature; they are at a level of existence lower than our own, and envelop us in living intertwining waves of colour, of weaving tones and of flowing spirituality.

By day, beings of the third elemental kingdom influence our astral body; those of the second get at our etheric body; and those of the first kingdom gain access to the physical body to destroy it. Only when in sleep the astral body works back on the physical body, protecting and caring for it, are these destructive processes made good. But we can only experience this world when we have devotion to it, the desire and urge to surrender ourself entirely to it. Love must hold sway in cognition.

The spiritual region lying behind nature, which consists only of forces of antipathy, holds together with centripetal force the physical world, which would otherwise disperse in all directions. This astral world that we enter at night is cold and icy, yet filled with wisdom; but we bring into it cosmic forces of love and soul-warmth from within our inner being. This is pre-eminently our cosmic task, for without these forces this region would disperse in dust. We would however pass really bad nights if we experienced this consciously.[28]

Whilst our soul is directly subject in sleep to the higher kingdoms of the universe, our physical and life bodies are subject to their cosmic-physical mirror images – only their influence is unhealthy. There live inside the surface of the earth, both in the solid and watery elements, pernicious beings akin to the helpers of Moon, Mercury and Venus, who scorned to go with Jehovah to the moon, and remain in these elements, persuading us while we sleep that evil is good and vice versa. These are Ahrimanic beings who would give us an etheric body to keep us permanently on earth (but seldom succeed). Similar irregular beings related to the outer planets inhabit the warmth and air, and seek to make us into moral automata, influenced by the stars but ignoring the earth. These are Luciferic beings, for example those underlying an outworn theology. This is extraordinarily complicated.[29]

We here enter a world which has the inclination to destroy the physical world of the senses, and our dreams are filled with its terribly destructive forces, their pictures destroy every shred of logic. If they were strong enough, these forces would seize also all our other instincts and our emotional life; they would destroy the whole life of physical human beings. On waking, the forces of our body, its powers of thought and ideas, again overcome these destructive forces. If you consider this properly, you will gain deep insight into the relationship between sleeping and waking.[30]

Part of the life spent in sleep is thus extraordinarily many-sided; it brings many people into contact with elemental beings of the cosmos connected with the lower passions and manifestations of human nature. In this kingdom people are up to all manner of queer practices which they are quite above following in outer life. Many frolic in bad elemental company! Who does not know what it is to be ashamed of one's dreams? (p120)

If one doses on a train journey, the ego and astral body are right inside all the rattling, rumbling and braking going on in the wheels and the engine of the train. They bring back with them what they experienced while they were being squeezed through the machinery right up to the moment of waking. The effect on the etheric body is really as though one's physical body was being bruised and dismembered. This is an absolutely unavoidable side-effect of modern life. Anthroposophy must help us to develop the force in heart and will to arm ourselves against such influences.

The modern human being who has been suffering from spiritual undernourishment since the last third of the nineteenth century is well-nigh absorbed by the spirituality of nature when his soul leaves the body – you should see what a ghastly, shrunken framework his soul becomes. He takes no spirituality with him because the intellect does not nourish the spirit.

When we descend too deeply into physical corporality we come into the realm of sub-nature, that of the Nether Gods, of the Father. And if the soul-spiritual entity goes too far in enhancing sleep to clairvoyance, we meet the Upper Gods,* the realm of the Spirit. Only when we have a normal relation between our soul and spirit and our body do we live in the natural world. If this sub-nature and super-nature are not kept in balance by sleep, body and soul illnesses respectively appear. Christ is the mediator in both worlds; He permeates and creates harmony both in nature and in our world of normal human existence.

9. Deeper Experiences

This first phase of sleep is inwardly vague, undifferentiated, with no difference between one's own being and the universe, nor between separate objects or people. Ego-feeling comes to include

---

* The First Hierarchy (Seraphim, Cherubim and Thrones) work from below; The Second Hierarchy (Kyriotetes, Dynamis and Exusiai/Elohim) and the Third Hierarchy (Archai, Archangels and Angels) from above.

universe-feeling. This state is still interwoven with dreams, making it still less clear to Imaginative consciousness. A strong sense of sequence is present, but all feeling of space is almost completely wiped out. We move about in a general indefinite world substance, like a wave in a universal sea, now here, now there. Earthly dimension, number and weight are not there at all. There is however an experience of relative size, even of relative number. Free-floating, free-moving sense perceptions – colours, sounds and so on – continue but have a counter weight, tending to scatter and escape into universal space.

If we become conscious when sight and hearing are no longer a mere chaotic mingling of colours and sounds, we begin to feel that things are ordered, and perception arises of spiritual beings who realise themselves within these free-floating sense experiences. We enter the life and doings of spiritual beings, we are with all that is spiritual in all the beings of nature. This is combined with an experience of being forsaken and alone, as if hovering over an abyss – were one to be conscious of it without the right preparation it would be quite unbearable.

We have to prepare for the feeling of having lost the support of our body, and endure the fear of facing something wholly unknown and indeterminate. Although the sleeper is not ordinarily conscious of such fear, he passes through delicate differences in certain vascular activities, which show that something objective happens. Were we to be fully conscious of the first moments – or in many cases, perhaps hours – after falling asleep, we would be filled with this fear. The anxiety sets going too a constant alternation between a state of inner tranquillity and one of uneasiness. It produces a profound unconscious yearning towards the divine which permeates the whole cosmos.

This in turn resolves itself into a kind of hovering, weaving, ever-moving cloud formation, in which we feel alive but in danger of becoming submerged. Rosicrucian mystery teaching explained that during these first experiences on going to sleep, when hovering in powerlessness and anxiety, yet filled with something like an inner force of gravity, the student of the new mysteries should raise into consciousness the words 'Ex Deo Nascimur'.* 31 The self must be made stronger than is necessary for ordinary life, and only when through exercises we have an excess of self-reliance do we no longer want to shrink back from higher worlds. But then a new and considerable danger arises, for we may bring forth this expanded and strengthened self-consciousness as boundless egoism.

This loss of security carries with it, however, the sense of being concealed and protected within divine spiritual reality. Deep longing arises for the divine-spiritual power which leads in waking life to religious feelings. We would never philosophise about how the individual is grounded and rooted in the cosmos, nor ever come to a feeling of God, were it not for this. The duration of sleep does not really matter for these experiences, for utterly different time conditions prevail in the spiritual world.

On losing even dream consciousness, Imagination shows that we then live in the formative forces of the universe, the universal thoughts. Our mental pictures are then no longer arbitrary, but such as those creatively active in world evolution, as described in *Occult Science* (although we can only perceive them if we have first acquired conscious knowledge of them). The etheric body assumes through its own principles a structure that images the universe in a truly magnificent way. It bears within it

* From God we are born.

everything that we received at birth from the universe, depending on how we lived between death and rebirth, and is alive and active in all we have experienced since our birth, structured by cosmic powers. All this radiates out from our etheric bodies during sleep.

This whole world of objective flowing thoughts – not concerned with our phantasy or memories – is always present, but by day it is drowned by our subjective thoughts of the outer world. Its objective weaving is not merely of thoughts, but also of forces of growth, nutrition and life in general. It is the first element of the life of the soul, and weaves within us, permeating our etheric body inwards and shaping our physical body outwards. It contains a much higher logic than our normal thinking, and even outlives the earth.[32]

When we go out of our body with feeling and will, we perceive this body of formative forces as a web of active thoughts, as though it were a mirror or photographic plate; it stands before us. This is similar to the miniature reflection of the world that we ordinarily have in our eye, but it is now reflected through the soul and spirit; we see not only the web of our own thoughts but also the world thoughts.* Then we first come to know the thoughts which the divine spiritual Beings have stored up, in order to pass beyond the life of nature and to work creatively on human beings. There are thus two quite different factors, the thoughts which enter via the impressions of daily life and those

---

* These world thoughts are the original growth forces of our body, but were debased by Lucifer at the Fall. They were, however, redeemed by Christ to become the 'incorruptible body' (1 Cor 15:42f) or 'phantom' (10.12.11f). But they are still permeated by the past karma of each individual. R.G.S.

memory thoughts which rise up from within. These are different currents of inner life; in every situation memories mingle with the momentary impressions made by life – during sleep they are also in evidence.

While we sleep a complete and tremendous activity takes place. We work over, for example, in our subsequent sleep, and perhaps the following nights, a lecture that we heard, and it would be possible to gather much more from this than even the lecturer himself knew. Even the inattentive would draw in the spiritual powers and impulses of the thoughts, which would be transformed into what we require even beyond death. Everything we experience by day we work on and learn from at night. The etheric body goes on thinking all through the night, united in movement with the whole universe. These thoughts are not then without life, although we are not present in them. Memories are also in evidence.

We can carry nothing into sleep from the concepts we evolve through outer observation, or through science or experiments; for the intellect does not nourish the spirit. We tear our astral body and ego away from the sense world which we comprehend with our intellect and sleep in nothingness. We are not nothing when we sleep, but instead we enter a world of the future which is as yet a nothing to us.[33]

Then at a certain moment the pictures of this stage of light sleep, which have become distinct and revealed the world thoughts behind them, fade away until nothing remains but a kind of feeling of these dying unconscious experiences.

10. Bodily Processes

In sleep the ego and astral body do not see the body as such, but see a hollow space surrounded by an aura which is more or less brilliant, as though in a fog or mist; the physical human being is an empty dark space inside it. Seen clairvoyantly during sleep, the physical and etheric bodies remind us of the centaur – the upper part bears the human face, in a very shadowy form; but the lower part, which appears stronger, even denser than our present form, reminds us of animal forms. These are the forces that draw us down during the day and lead us astray into personal interests.

The sunlight preserved within the ego and astral body by day shines down on to the body, and not only irradiates the skin but is directed through the *senses* to the nervous system, flooding it with light. Meanwhile the ever-changing moon forces also work within the physical and etheric bodies, stimulating the etheric processes. These together generate sufficient freshness, growth forces and vitality to prevent the body from drying up, withering and fading; but it is not enough to restore the damage done to the organism by day.

Part of the sentient body remains connected with the etheric body during sleep. Hence we are subject to exactly the same sense impressions as by day e.g. warmth, hearing, touch – except that the eyes are closed. Thus apart from sight, the sense-impressions are not held back by the physical organism. Inspiration shows that the sense organs are like gulfs extended into us by the outside world, and sleep is a kind of enhancement of the surrender of the senses to the world. The sense organs themselves are actually most awake during sleep – were the eyes not asleep while we are awake we could see nothing. Neither are the thoughts held back, they continually stream through the body, although we are not conscious of them. We sleep and dream continuously on the outer surface of the body, but we cannot completely understand our sensations (which are feeling-will) until our intellect comprehends them by day.

The equilibrium of our *breathing* rhythm arises from forces lying outside the chest. On the one hand the rhythm is influenced by everything taking place in the head and on the other by everything taking place in the metabolism. The organisation of the head in its entire development follows a much slower tempo than the metabolic limb organism, approximately 1:4 (i.e the pulse beats four times to one breath). In sleep, the number of breaths is reduced, the carbon dioxide content of the outbreath being reduced by about a quarter.* Inwardly, everything Ahrimanic has the tendency towards the slow head rhythm, which hardens the forms and makes them pointed and rigid. In everything Luciferic, the fast bodily rhythm predominates, which rounds everything off, because it runs its course faster. In this rounding, the forms are not made rigid but wave-like.

When outside the body we become extremely partial to the outbreath; our soul and spirit in fact breathe in spiritually the impressions made by the exhaled carbon dioxide. The air thus maintaining connection with the physical body brings us continually the secrets of our inner life, so that as it sparkles forth we feel: that am I myself. Our own spirit streaming towards us in the exhaled air has a sun-like appearance, it appears luminous against the darkness behind; objective world thoughts appear in

---

* Consistent with the slowing in sleep of most functions of the autonomic nervous system (p15).

it – it is felt as an outer world. Only in Inspiration does this become conscious.[34]

We can comprehend our soul world as woven into the rhythm of the airy element, for that is where it reveals itself. In sleep we do not work on the air organism, but allow the cosmic astrality to draw into it. We similarly allow the cosmic spirit to draw into our warmth organism. The inhalation process continuously creates the human being. It inhales formative forces appropriate to one's being and is activated by day by our own astral body, but during the night the cosmic astrality controls the breathing. We have a perpetual human birth in the element of air in the inhalation process. The air exhalation partakes in the metabolic activity prior to leaving the body.

Throughout life there is also a second finer breathing process centred primarily in the head. When the will is no longer active in the senses, the etheric body becomes all the more active and inwardly mobile; from the places where the sense-organs are located, a continual lively etheric activity streams inwards. This occurs in the elemental warmth, into which plays the entire cosmic etheric world – the warmth element is taken in via the senses and the whole surface of the skin, bringing with it light, chemical/sound and life ethers.* From the moment of falling asleep a particular process originates from the region of the eyes as if, through the influence of light whilst awake, the eye had stored up forces for an activity that develops only when asleep. As light and colour from outside darken, the eyes themselves begin, like two phosphorescent suns, to irradiate the interior of

* The etheric world is fourfold, consisteing of warmth, light, chemical/sound and life ethers – corresponding broadly to fire, air, water and solid states of the physical world.

the physical part of the sleeper with a phosphorescent, glimmering light. The light ether stays behind within the head, and floods the human being with inner light, which becomes the nightly thought activity.

The remaining ethers, 'exhaled' from the head through the *nerve-sense process*, unite with the forces of the inhaled air, and are carried to the point where inhalation borders on exhalation in normal breathing. Here the chemical/sound ether stops, stimulating the forces of the rhythmic system – our feeling organisation. A kind of humming and singing, a changing murmur within the organism, continues as music extraordinarily rich in melody, and harmony fills the whole interior from which the ego and astral body receive strong impressions. The life ether is however carried further by exhalation activated by the etheric body, until it is taken up by the metabolism where it becomes our organism that wills. With much else difficult to describe, there results an immeasurably beautiful and impressive living and streaming of the etheric body.[35]

If on going to sleep we can look back into the etheric body of the *head*, we see the products of the plant and animal kingdoms carried up by the blood and nervous system to nourish the brain. But in a small, vital and most noble part of the brain, the etheric body allows only the mineral extract of plants to contact the purest extract of light, heat and sound from the senses. This is where the man of thought is sustained. This is depicted in the Grail legend.[36]

At night the activity of the ego and astral body on the nervous system of the brain, which connects with the entire etheric body, becomes quiescent. But the brain cells become restless, and we become unconscious (p41). The strength required to increase the brain activity is withdrawn from other areas of the body, in particular from some of the white blood cells, which become less lively. As a result we should actually begin to think with our body. Can we think at night with liver, stomach and other organs, perhaps even with the intestines? If we awoke too suddenly we should perceive the most marvellous thoughts in our body. But the breathing process blurs this and gives rise to dreams.

Upon the *lower organism* the action of the ego and astral body is all the more vigorous, and is strongly bound up with the metabolic process; it has less significance for the chest organs. In sleep the spinal nervous system becomes more intimately connected with the astral body; and the autonomic system, which extends throughout the trunk ensheathing the spinal cord with its fibres, becomes more strongly connected with the actual 'I'. But the 'I' is still too young to bring what it experiences in the autonomic system to consciousness; the instrument is too delicate, though its life is no less significantly vivid.

In sleep the nervous and blood systems would indeed be destroyed, were it not that in proportion as the ego and astral withdraw a divine astral body and ego are seen clairvoyantly to flow in. The body becomes the bearer or temple of higher Beings who guard and protect it. This divine astral body and ego are in fact active also by day, but are then overpowered by our own.

In our physical/life body, the worn-out nervous system and the etheric body begin to manifest a plant-like activity – they begin to bud and blossom. The moment of going to sleep must be compared with the spring, and the deeper our sleep the more do our physical and etheric bodies pass over into a condition of sprouting life. They become subject to the processes of the mineral and plant kingdoms respectively; but these are not at all suited to the body's constitution. Spiritual life can only unfold on the basis of catabolic (breaking-down) processes, and these must go on even in sleep (alongside the restorative anabolic activity) so that one's soul and spiritual life as a whole can unfold. If the catabolic processes are not to cause illnesses they must be brought into balance – there must be just as much of them as is needed for waking life next morning; too much accumulation of catabolic residue causes illness. Thus the same processes are the basis for both spiritual development and illness. Unfortunately, the etheric body also contains all the bad and destructive elements that our ego and astral body have implanted into it during life.

Although the astral and the ego-organization* are not directly active on the body during sleep, substances taken hold of by their day's activities continue to work on, as though by inertia; and the body is taken hold of from within by the forces of these substantial residues. Substances taken in during both waking and sleeping act differently; for example, oxygen in waking life battles against the soporific influence of oxygen absorption, but when the astral body's work is suspended it unfolds its inherent nature and sends us to sleep. Fats too behave differently when the ego and astral body are withdrawn. They are not worked on in sleep, but deposited as bodily fat, providing warmth. If someone 'sleeps' while awake, excess fat is laid down, and a pot belly develops.

* The ego-organisation is the sum of patterns and forces that works in blood and bone as foundation for the I-consciousness, either consciously or unconsciously. It is a purely qualitative reality that cannot be pictured.

11. The Beginnings of Karma

The moral order on earth is bound up with our etheric body, so that when we pass into sleep we leave our moral achievements with our etheric body in bed, and are not armed with our moral qualities. However, for Imagination, a memory of our moral attitude, of our qualities of soul, arises particularly vividly just after going to sleep, and gradually passes away toward waking. The motives of the will in our ordinary actions pass into our organisation; but we also press out a whole sum of will impulses into the purely spiritual world (p93). What we have done through the day, whether good or bad, viewing it to begin with according to customary ideas, begins immediately to be integrated into the stream of karmic development. This process continues for a time and at first overshadows everything else.

This stream of impressions of daily life is now reversed; we undergo what the other person experienced as a consequence of our action, their physical pain or moral suffering. But this is still *only a picture*, not yet reality. We retrace the life of the past day in reverse order, one person in one minute, another in five. If disturbed, the rest of the time can be retraced almost instantaneously. We live through our experiences inwardly, and far more intensively, seriously and significantly than by day. Through our ego and soul, we ourselves examine and judge their value and import within the whole world connection. An immensely deep, inner conscientiousness permeates this activity, which of course remains unconscious.

The essences of the day's entire experiences, taken directly into those spheres where the soul or inner human being resides, converge and coalesce into a new faculty, as is apparent when learning to write. They are drawn together into unity, as if woven into a fabric, and emerge as abilities, wisdom or art, life experience or love for one another. For this to happen, our entire range of daily experiences must become united with the soul and be worked on by it during sleep.[37]

Young children copy what is around them, each gesture or movement is of moral significance, even a person's thoughts are perceived. But the remarkable thing is that during sleep the child makes a choice; what he wants to absorb he sends into his physical organism, what he does not is ejected into the etheric world; thus he takes in only what is predestined by his karma.[38]

On falling asleep we strike up against that which cannot become deed – the untransformed impulses of will and feeling. Everything in the soul life that does not pass into deed is future karma.[39] As we live through the day in reverse we prepare future karma in the pictures, which are still very bungling. These pictures cannot as yet adapt to the physical body properly, and must be adjusted with the help of the Beings of the Higher Hierarchies, when forming the spirit germ for the next life on earth. After death it is the nights that supply the foundation in the soul world for the way we must cope with our past experiences with others.

Then at a certain moment the pictures of this stage of light sleep, which have become distinct and revealed the world thoughts behind them, fade away until nothing remains but a kind of feeling of these dying unconscious experiences.

IV SECOND PHASE OF SLEEP

12. Body and Soul

We no longer participate in the processes of bodily life alone, but are concerned with a world common to both body and soul. Elements connected with the body play over into the soul. We find ourselves as beings of soul, not as we now are but as we were before conception; we learn to know how we lived between death and rebirth – this belongs to this second stage of sleep. We invariably go back through time to the moment when we descended from heavenly realms to earth. The etheric body alone forms the only connection across life to the age of the physical, containing the whole of our life from the time we were born.

Inspiration shows how, even during the shortest sleep, the ego experiences again in reverse order everything gone through whilst last awake, together with the judgment – made now by the whole spiritual cosmos – as to whether an action, thought or feeling is good or bad. This remains unconscious until experienced again after death during kamaloca.* We also experience at this stage all the human souls that we have contacted during life. Everything we experience between death and new birth also plays right into our life of feeling and will – into what we sleep and dream through. This creates our feelings and moods of happiness and unhappiness by day. It leads intuitively to the certainty of reincarnation, to other spirits who never

* The 'place of desires', lasting about one third of earthly life.

incarnate, to our good and evil tendencies, and to predestined events. In fact, karma is now presented to the soul.

Inspiration realises too that in sleep we live unconsciously as a cloud of weaving, living light in cosmic light. This means living in forces that in waking life are grasped in thoughts. But the light is permeated with forces that work creatively in nature, it is the body of spiritual weaving and of each spiritual being. We also live as substance of warmth in the cosmic warmth which permeates the light. This we perceive as weaving strength-giving love. As beings of love we live among beings who draw love out of their own essence.[40]

When we awaken spiritually during sleep, we first see what relates to ourselves, the creative life-giving principles working in us. It really seems as if the processes of the kingdoms of nature were blotted out and the earth contained only humanity.

All the instreaming phosphorescent light, sound, etc within the etheric body is now seen as the external clothing, the revelation, the glory of mighty cosmic Beings, the Spirits of Form. Moreover, these streams become further inwards an organically coherent system, a shell-like copy of the human being, which consists of flowing thought-forms of the cosmos, but now individualised – the individualised Logos. This speaks a silent language, an inner word, repeating all we have said from evening to morning, and revealing the whole nature of the soul. At the same time, even during a nap, it writes the occult script into the time-sequence of the etheric world in the gleaming, gently phosphorescent light. (The result is known as the Akashic record, which can be researched by the initiate.) Here the Spirits of Movement are active.[41]

The soul-being of the sun (meaning the countless spiritual beings who populate it) weaves sun-Imaginations. Imaginative forces which play upon the plants are particularly active in spring, and our soul then lives and weaves outside the body in this element. In summer sleep the Upper Gods come down, and we live with our soul and spirit within the sharply contoured cosmic Imaginations pressed near to the earth. In winter sleep the Nether Gods ascend, and the meshes of the cosmic Imaginations widen out, leading our ego and astral body to far distances of the universe; the windows of earth open, and Archangels and Angels behold what we actually are in our feelings.

When we fall asleep we also plunge with our lower astral aura into what we call the astral body of the earth – an order of spiritual beings called the Spirits of the Cycles of Time. They have command over the nature spirits, allotting their work to the seasons, and bring about day and night, everything connected with rhythmic alternation. Their activity is not merely life-giving but resembles the action of feeling and thought on our souls; we are merged into them and they influence our astral body. Everything in their realm is fundamentally multiplicity, plurality; if we are still asleep in our ego yet awake in our astral body, we feel dismembered in their world. Behind the Spirits of the Cycles of Time lives the Planetary Spirit of our planet Earth itself with which we are united.

The ego changes all the time during sleep as it moves through the cosmic 'I', becoming more unconscious until a climax is reached, and then slowly it becomes more conscious again. The result of this ego rhythm is the revolution of the earth.[42] The actual upbuilding forces of the earth planet lie in humankind, not in the single individual. If no human beings were asleep on earth, the vegetative powers of the earth would die down much more rapidly than they actually do. Human beings do not exist just for their own sake; our sleep has cosmic significance. The consciousness at work here is at the level of life spirit.*

The physical and etheric bodies now appear as though enlarged into a world connected with the whole earth, like a plant awakening in spring, growing and greening. Mineral and vegetable life bud in them, though naturally in a quite different way. These plants appear very beautiful when seen asleep, like a whole earth shooting and sprouting. It is, however, as if the roots penetrated from above, the flowers and fruit growing into our body; it is completely upside down. The fruits express the strengthening brought by sleep. We behold elemental forces coming from the cosmos; substantial Beings, not only elemental beings, are active. We get the impression too that our astral body is gnawing away at the roots, as the animal eats the plants. What the astral body makes its own is the harvest of life, which we take through the gate of death.

13. Solar and Planetary Experiences

Another mood develops, in which we feel: I would fain rest in the bosom of the Godhead – that is, rest in the blessings of the spirals over the meadow. If this experience of devotion to the divine were not carried over into waking life, our nourishment by

---

* Spirit self, life spirit and spirit man represent three higher stages of human development, awaiting transformation by the 'I' of the astral, etheric and physical bodies respectively – see *Occult Science* (5).

day would assume a completely earthly character and throw our organism into disorder. The upper astral aura (with the ego now enclosed within it) uses these spirals circling above every plant (which carry the forces regulating its growth) as a ladder by which to send threads, currents, tentacles towards the great astral universe. Though not expanded into the whole planetary cosmos, it is diffused and enlarged to true cosmic existence, moving as a cloud in spiral form.

When Inspiration begins we become aware, as if through a sudden jolt of soul and spirit, that we have arrived with our upper aura within the sun, which now becomes our eye and ear and our organ of warmth. Our being is within the light, we feel that we are within the sun's linear path. This is where our soul goes in ordinary sleep.[43] It radiates its currents to the planetary Beings of Mercury, Mars, Jupiter and so on, in whom are the strengthening powers needed. The powers that drive Jupiter – the Spirits of Wisdom – working on the rational soul are those, above all, that strengthen us.

The part of the astral body which belongs in waking life to the heart becomes a 'heart-eye' or 'heart ear' for a very dim experience (of which dreams may still catch a glimpse). This 'eye' looks back to the body in bed, and the etheric body reflects to it pictures of the planetary movements. We experience it all in our astral body in a sort of planetary globe; these astral images constitute our inner organism. (There are circulations of planetary movements in astral substance, just as by day the blood courses through our physical organism.)

The life of our soul is now a solar system in miniature. We carry within us these little pictures, different for each of us, in which the planetary movements are reproduced – for example the relation between the movements of Jupiter and Venus may shed light on our gifts and talents, our inclination to good and evil. And we should in general not be able to think intelligently unless we received into our breathing and blood circulation during the day the after-effects of the planetary experiences during the night; the powers of wisdom and ingenuity arise from this. Such experiences are intimately connected with our destiny. We follow with our astral body all that happens there. It seems to us as though the single parts of our entity were divided up into the whole planetary universe; but what we really undergo is only a division between the counterparts of the stars that we carry within us during our entire earth life.

Nevertheless, our soul does split up its life into many parts, and fear again arises, because the soul has immersed itself into an enormous number of separate beings of soul and spirit, and is actually manifold. Suppose the relationship between Jupiter and Venus is raying back from our etheric body; one ray is reflected from the forehead, another from below the heart, which mingles its music and light with the first. This gives rise to anxiety and apprehension of a spiritual nature, we feel we are becoming as dim and nebulous as a cosmic mist. Into the anxiety must flow power gained from religious or similar experiences the day before; when these are blended and intermingled they give rise to a reviving and refreshing force which streams into the organism for the coming day.

We feel the need for guidance; but this only appears if we have created a bond with Christ, who must be conceived here as connected with the life of the sun. The Rosicrucian pupil was taught: In Christo Morimur. The soul must perish, should it not die into cosmic life in Christ.[44] Christ performed his deed on

Golgotha to rescue human bodies from decay, irrespective of what other people believe. But to take effect in the spirit and soul in freedom, he must be able to penetrate the soul whilst independent of the body in sleep. This is only possible for an individual who consciously acknowledges the Mystery of Golgotha. The soul-saving effect corresponds to self-surrender to Christ, the religious experience in the contemplation of His life, death and Being. The leadership of Christ overcomes soul-fear, and transforms the plurality to unity. Really to feel 'Not I, but Christ in me' gives us our bearings in the labyrinth of planetary movements.

Thus in our ego and astral body we are really one with the life forces of sun and stars, the great world forces to which we return at death; but we have liberated ourselves from them, and are independent of our true home, so that we can sleep even when the sun is shining. The Higher Beings who enter into our body at night have their scene of activity generally speaking on the sun, but the conditions of space do not apply to them, so they can nevertheless send their forces into our physical body.

When the pictures of the first stage rise up again in an alternation of activity and withdrawal, something else appears which can be called the harmony of the spheres, cosmic music. This reveals itself as the deeds and activities of the Third Hierarchy and so on – the revelations of cosmic spiritual beings. Having discarded the pictures of Imagination, we experience in Inspiration an inward ringing sound, and in the cosmic weaving of arising and vanishing Imaginations we behold the actions and deeds of the beings of the Hierarchies, and move around them.

While we sleep the soul thus absorbs in spiritland the world of tones, the impressions of which are followed by a musical person's physical nature, though they may not know it.

Musical pleasure is based on the right accord between these harmonies and the tones and melodies on earth. To be musically gifted means to have an astral body sensitive by day to what whirrs through it the whole night long, the instreaming of tones from the world of Archangels. Something comparable may be said of the other arts. Music is concerned with time and the inner worlds, whereas the formative arts imitate forms of waking consciousness, space and the outside world.

In this deeper dreamless sleep, forces of the astral body reach as far as the starry world, where the soul-beings of the plants are to be found, and it draws its strength from that world. The astral body now reposes in a world where the stars are embedded – the world of the harmony of the spheres, according to the Pythagoreans. If we live consciously in this world, we can hear the stars resounding in their reciprocal forces and relations. It is accessible only to Inspiration, and is one-dimensional.

We must 'feel' in quite a concrete way the spiritual world into which we are submerged when we fall asleep; we must feel and know how there lives there what is now happening as a result of the mission entrusted by Christ to Michael, inasmuch as Michael has been exalted from Folk Spirit to Time Spirit.[45]

14. The Work of the Third Hierarchy

On rising into the actual world of the Hierarchies, we feel as though we belong there. All is 'being', we experience the nature of the Beings. Our soul is bound up with a thought and we cannot distinguish the thought from ourself; we have to say: a thought thinks itself in me, we are one with the Beings and we experience their experience. We feel our whole nature poured out into the sphere in which they live.

The astral body and ego could not repair the exhausted forces if they themselves were not taken up into the realm of the Third Hierarchy and other Beings. It is as if a spiritual ozone streamed through them, from which the astral body absorbs the forces required. From the time of going to sleep to that of waking we are in the elemental world, and from there we look out now into the expanses of the superelemental world of the Third Hierarchy – although unless in childhood we learnt of the spiritual world we cannot make a real connection with these Beings.

Deep reverence fills us when in Imagination we see the Third Hierarchy, in mighty spirit-clouds over our body, wending their way to all that unfolds in our etheric body, and we become aware how we create work for them. All that we have thought by day begins to move and ring on waves of sound. Those beings who hover over us – Angels, Archangels and Archai, rising and descending, busy themselves with traces of the thoughts in our etheric body that remain as an echo of the day.

If the Angels did not work into our ego and astral body in sleep, we should never feel ourselves to be free personalities. Because the Archangels work into us, we can feel ourselves as members of the whole of humanity. And because the Archai, the Time Spirits, pulsate in our nature, filling it with Intuition, we feel part of earthly humanity from the beginning to the end of earth evolution. (We try to evoke this by speaking of the cultural ages, led by the Time Spirits, in which consciousness alters and develops.)

Our astral body is in fact an outgrowth from the Angels (as is our etheric from the Archangels and our physical from the Archai). Hence the Angel is obliged in a sense to accompany us in sleep. He always goes with children, but with adults it depends on an affinity in the intimate depths of soul. If we cultivate only material thoughts he does not accompany us, for he would deny his fellowship with the Archangels and higher Beings were he to do so. This question whether during sleep we are able to partake of the presence of our Angel is one of the most important in human life, showing that we are an important part of the whole cosmic system. If the Angel does not accompany us, we bring back Ahrimanic inspirations – the whole of materialistic thought then emerges from sleep.[46] If by day our thoughts contain idealism, a relation is found to the Angels who nurture our thought forces, which we cannot do for ourselves; they gather these fruits, and in sleep bear them out into the cosmos.

Awakened consciousness can perceive the light active during sleep in building up the eyes: extending and contracting the lens in the form of an Angel projected from oneself in the spirit world sweeping towards the body; and the blood caring for the eyes as an Archangel battling to conquer the demons of darkness – Archangels have for generations of gods worked on the eye.

Astral body and ego, moreover, take into sleep everything of a soul nature, the soul impulses that we have by day put into speech. Something streams back into the soul, where it echoes in reverse sequence – the undulation of feeling, the will-impulses, the gaiety or sadness, joy or pain in the flow of speech. This must echo in such a way that Archangels can take pleasure in it; before puberty it is instead what is heard from the hearts and souls of those around that echoes. If ideals are not embodied, if words do not have wings, we may be chained in sleep to the physical. Language today fetters the soul and no longer enables the clear speech of Angels and the resounding trumpet tones of Archangels, with their deep significance, to be heard. Every soul lives in sleep where all folk souls act, lives within their dance, except for the one folk soul in which we live whilst awake. But if we feel a particular hatred for one or several, we are forced to live with those.

The forces which call forth the movements of our will are nurtured by the Archai. One who puts idealism into his actions relates rightly to the Archai. Through the echo of daily work the 'I' is carried to the Archai, which gives us the force to control to a certain extent the impulses of the physical body, ensuring that there is no hindrance in doing what we decide in freedom of thought. True human love, universal and unselfish, sincere in interest in everyone we meet, alone connects us rightly with the Archai; while the ego rests in their bosom, karma is shaped, reaching to the next life.

It is under the influence of light that processes of destruction take place by day in our physical body. On Ancient Saturn there was as yet no light, its activity on the physical body was upbuilding. Therefore it was necessary for certain Saturn beings to be held back, so that they could rebuild the physical body during sleep, when there is no light. The Spirits of Form must interweave the work of these beings of darkness into their own work, or there could be no stability in cosmic activity. To this day the backward Archai Beings of Ancient Saturn are active in us during sleep, when they work upon our physical and etheric bodies, building them up.[47]

While we sleep, Angels, Archangels and Archai live in the pulsation of the blood (in which our ego lives when we are awake); and when our astral body leaves our organs of breathing, Spirits of Form (Elohim), of Movement and of Wisdom (the

Second Hierarchy) work there. These Spirits send their messengers or helpers during sleep to give our human form the right expression. Helpers of the Spirits of Form nurture our ego; others sent by them, and by the Spirits of Movement, the guardians of our ego, work on our thinking; those of the Spirits of Wisdom work on our heart and the blood circulation; other elemental beings work on the spiritual warmth arising from our human relationships; others again work behind the vowels and consonants of the word sense. Innumerable elementary beings form the marvellous temple of the body.

V THIRD PHASE OF SLEEP

15. Relating to the Fixed Stars

The third condition of sleep lifts us wholly out of our bodies and places us in the spiritual world itself, but at this stage the soul has no relation to what is taking place in the body. The images of the fixed stars are within us – we really become cosmic beings. The ordinary view of the cosmos ceases, the whole starry world vanishes, and from its rays come forth the genii, the spirits, the gods of the stars. However, it certainly does happen that we have nights when we only go through the two previous phases.

In the third phase the astral body uses the forces that carry the plant upright to reach the zodiac, it expands and is spread abroad through the whole starry world, attracting towards itself the purest cosmic forces.* Only from actually being within the world of soul and spirit can we draw out the health-giving forces. Half an hour after falling asleep, or somewhat later, we feel ourselves within the twelve constellations, living within the Beings of the fixed stars. We feel the relationships between the activities of these Beings, and go through a copy or imitation of them. Meanwhile our limited ego descends into the cosmic 'I' and fore-goes its own activity, so that the cosmic 'I' can work unhindered. Every night we must unconsciously obliterate at the boundary of the higher spiritual world the memory of all our past.

* On passing from the mobility of the planets to the fixed star patterns, electrical frequency falls from 12-14hz to 2-4hz (p13).

Only through Intuition do we fully understand that during sleep we go still further out with our soul into the sphere beyond the sun, so that we must perceive only through the sun. The part of the astral body which permeates the solar plexus and the whole limb system is now an additional organ of perception which may be called a 'sun eye'. With this 'sun-eye' we begin to feel the forces in our astral body coming from the zodiac – it makes a great difference whether they come directly or through the earth. This realm beyond the sun has a powerful influence on our soul nature (knowledge of this was once depicted by the halo).

The forces expressed in our arms and legs arise from this region, which we also enter between death and rebirth. This is the world of all the nine Hierarchies, who can only contact the natural world through the human being. Thus we are not a unity, but the confluence of two spiritual domains; we are embedded in the whole cosmos.[48] We become aware of this stage occasionally when we wake with a sense of having undergone very profound experiences and with a sense of heaviness that must be overcome during the next few hours. Its content can only be grasped by Intuition, yet it is of great significance.

If our planetary and fixed star experience during sleep were to be conscious, we should have a cosmology full of content, and conclude that we have a life as spirit among spirits. To Intuition the cosmic experience of the soul widens, and this experience reverberates by day as religious leanings and longings. Imagination, Inspiration and Intuition show how we really are part of the cosmos, and how we become one with God.

As before, anxiety comes over us: what if I lose myself in the multitude of stars and manifold happenings? If this anxiety felt in our astral body and ego were not carried over into the body as a force, we should not be able to hold together our physical constitution or secrete salts and similar substances in the way necessary for the organism. It is exceedingly difficult to attain clarity regarding this complicated experience; we need to do so, but we hardly can without a heart-understanding of all that Christ willed to become for the earth. But if we have once thought and felt about this, the astral body can receive via the body a certain tincture or quality through which Christ becomes our guide and leader through the zodiac, pointing the way from constellation to constellation. He brings order into these bewildering events.

With our 'sun-eye' we behold our karma (sec.19) – but all that is left of this in waking life is a kind of faint echo vibrating in the feelings. We have an afterworking, a faithful copy only, of our share in the being of the universal cosmos in our daily experience of light; but the feelings and after-effects of our cosmic experience must remain silent by day, so that we may unfold individual consciousness undisturbed by the heavenly world.

The astral body is not itself spatial but it works upon the spatial; it is in a sense part of the celestial universe, bringing order and organisation into the spatial through the differentiated lines of force from the zodiac. We find within the human body the direct working of these celestial powers, or their absence due to the earth's interference. And we become receptive to them in turn during sleep, including the continuing sleep of all inner physical processes which remain under the influence of the super-physical throughout life. The very young child, still supple and in a state of formation, is more or less always partially asleep, and consequently influenced much more than the adult.[49]

In the middle of almost every long sleep we experience
an inner union with the spirit self which we have yet to develop,
that is, with the qualities from which it will be extracted – a
meeting with our genius, of like nature to the Angels. All the
feelings that gladden the soul regarding the spiritual world
proceed from this, and through spiritual science souls will soon
be able to observe its effects, provided we observe the holiness of
sleep. The physical and etheric bodies are permeated during
sleep by divine spiritual Beings of the nature of spirit man and
life spirit. Thus the divine Beings who originally built our bodies
into such a magnificent, perfect temple occupy it again at night;
otherwise these bodies would perish.

During sleep, the Cosmic Will streams into us as the
power of activity, of which we know a weak copy when we move
our limbs. From the endless reservoir of Cosmic Feeling, the
light needed for inner experience streams into us in sleep,
through which the astral body is felt as reality. And from the
invisible world of Cosmic Thinking comes order and harmony as
a regulator between the power of movement and that of inner
light. We come to know this when we can experience consciously
the entry into the etheric body and physical body on waking.

In the etheric body, in its system of individualised
cosmic thought-forms (p64) we find towards the front of the
body a confluence known as 'the opposite vertebral column'. This
is a formation which permeates and integrates the lotus flowers,*
and is a manifestation of the Spirits of Wisdom. The weaving
together of the Spirits of Form, of Movement and of Wisdom is
the ultimate reality of the etheric body, which exists in the astral
body but manifests in the etheric. Particularly during sleep this

---

* Organs of spiritual perception – see *Occult Science* (5).

impressive etheric organ is revealed in its gleaming and glowing, its resonating and its manifold effects of warmth.[50]

Ego and astral body vanish into the worlds of the Spirits of Will and of Wisdom, building there, free of all errors and vices, centres of attraction for the substances needed, forces which have to flow from the world of Wisdom into the etheric body and from the world of Will into the physical body.

In sleep we rush through the cosmos in our ego and astral body much more actively than we go about in physical life, although we are not conscious of it. It is the Thrones that help us to do so. The First Hierarchy – Seraphim, Cherubim and Thrones – remain permanently in our etheric body, even while we are awake; and the powers of Father, Son, and Holy Spirit indwell our physical body. But they can only be recognised after the Christ impulse is received. The Word or Logos which was active from the beginning in the physical body is still active there today when that is deserted by the ego.

When we are *completely* asleep, astral body and ego-being abandon even the metabolic-limb system. We already experience at night a future time when we shall feel ourselves to be in the sun and moon and stars, and will look down from the cosmos on to the earth very differently from today.* Then the time comes when a feeling of timelessness arises, as though we were in a world that is round, without beginning or end. We are never really at rest there, and long to come somewhere to an end, to re-enter time.

We should be drawn still further out than the constellations of fixed stars, were it not for the moon, whose influence we

---

* This is the reality of a fourth phase of sleep, distinct from the arbitrary division by scientists (p13).

dimly divined even in the first phase. Now we begin to become acutely sensible of how moon forces hold us back within the world of the zodiac. They draw us away from the zodiac into experience of the planets and thence into those of the earth, taking us back through the same intermediate stages of sleep into the physical body and our animal nature. The moon forces also shine either directly or through the earth in a spiritual manner, but consideration of this and of its phases would take us into much finer and more subtle distinctions.

16. Relating to Physical Processes

Living in the images of the constellations that are within us, we learn now to know the sun as a fixed star in its constellation in relation to other constellations such as those of the zodiac. The stimulation given by this experience is required for the breathing and circulatory processes, enfired by the planets, to nourish and permeate our whole organism. This may seem a most materialistic activity, but our dependence on soul and spirit in the way this or that substance circulates in us is connected with the highest heavens. Thus by night the constellations constitute our inner being, we each become in truth a cosmic being. Experience of the fixed stars shoots by way of the metabolism, the transformation of our foods, into our life of day, without which the nutriment would not enter our brain in such a way that we can unfold initiative in our thought.[51]

Unlike the heart, the human brain has very little to do directly with solar activities on the earth but is much more concerned with the cosmic processes working beyond the solar system. During sleep our external nourishment can deeply influence the cosmic activities in the brain. Unsuitable food taken by day will affect the brain – thus the moment of waking is tremendously important for perception of whether one's digestion is in harmony with or in opposition to cosmic laws outside the solar system.[52]

The process of thinking is a salt-depositing process and the salt formed by our thinking must be dissolved by sleep, got rid of, otherwise it would induce destructive processes. In the re-dissolving of the deposits, beneficent sleep allows us ever anew to develop conscious thought by day. But we must constantly prevent the images from solidifying, and there is a certain force, to be found particularly in nitrogen, which can dissolve them. If we are not strong enough to do so, thus losing this ability to comprehend the images, the nitrogen level can be raised by increasing our protein intake. Sleepiness means that we cannot dissolve these images sufficiently and are overcome by the forces of sedimentation.

During sleep, inverted replicas are created in us of the happenings in the universe. The cosmos wants to create in us all kinds of forms of the inanimate mineral realm – we copy the cosmos, where everything is arranged as it is in crystals. We are completely merged in the mineral kingdom. With our souls we live in the inner being of the mineral world in spirit land, experiencing both its form and its inner forces, namely within the essential being of Angels, Archangels and other divine Beings. We thus understand what happens inside minerals and find our way into the essential nature of the higher Hierarchies. Deep sleep is felt on waking as a complete renewal; for we have dived down with full strength into the mineral processes working in us.

The ego and astral body 'sleep' in the radiations streaming upwards from the metals in the earth and in the influences which pour down from the moving planets and the constellations. The forces coming from the interior of the earth are localised in the organs of the upper body, while the forces that pour into the earth from the cosmos are localised in the organs of the lower body. There must be a regulated rhythm for each individuality between these two sets of forces, which manifests in a proper alternation between sleeping and waking.

It might be said, and not in a figurative sense, that by day we eat earth substance and by night take in what the stars and their activities give us. Albumen, for example, is worked on in sleep by the whole planetary system and the world of fixed stars. The soul is directly related to the Beings of the Hierarchies of whom the sun, moon and stars are the physical mirror images, and the body is subject to these cosmic-physical mirror images.[53]

Today the Gods carry out their activity in the metabolic-limb organism while we sleep. But the metabolic-limb system remains unconscious while we are awake, so the results of their work do not enter our thoughts. For example, the will reveals itself in the physical body as instinct, in the etheric body as drive, in the astral body as desire and in the ego as motive, but these are not recognised as divine spiritual deeds. Such truths reveal themselves only on the other side of the threshold.

The circulation of the blood, unconscious within us in waking life, begins in sleep to be very conscious, appearing as a new world before us; in the warmth processes connected with it we perceive the real 'I' working from past lives.

This real 'I' is connected physically by day with the lower part of the body, which is always asleep; it actually dwells in all the bodily activities which culminate in the formation of the blood from within. By night it is at its highest stage of spirituality, when most of the spirit is outside, but present already in what will develop in a later epoch. This meeting with the spiritual world strengthens our whole spiritual being, it is to a degree a self-understanding, a sizing up of ourselves. When such things live in our inner sentiments we shall have a definite and positive idea of the Grace of the Holy Spirit. Only because of a subconscious memory of this nightly experience are we not by day given entirely to materialistic thinking.[54]

Pastoral peoples of earlier times slept under the dark sky, from which came calmness and sleep; and where one of the countless stars shone down they became a little excited inside, and from their body a ray of oxygen went out to meet the star's ray. Each became an inner oxygen-mirror image of the whole starry firmament. They really felt the whole heavens inside them as images – ram, bull and so on. We still develop this, purely through inheritance, to give us strength – though now grown pale and thin. But today the task of spiritual science is to enable us to recognise in full consciousness the working of the divine spiritual deeds within ourselves.

If from deepest sleep we can look back clairvoyantly on our physical organs, the cosmic thoughts which flow into us would reveal them as the last decadent product of an absolute splendour now dead and shrivelled – the lungs as a formerly mighty picture of an eagle, the heart that of a lion, the lower part of the trunk as that of a bull, and around them almost all earthly animal forms. The nervous system appears as a number of wonderful plant-like beings embedded in the etheric body. Then Lucifer appears in the garden and the clairvoyant becomes aware of how in the far distant past the human being united himself with him. And self-knowledge reveals the astral body as an absolute egoist, who has brought about this decadence. As a result the higher Hierarchies pressed the human essence out through the senses to live outside this shrunken structure, which has now become the physical body.[55]

17. Morality and Sleep

Only the 'I' can be truly moral. The astral body may receive moral impulses only in so far as morality is carried over to it from the 'I' in the course of life. They cannot, however, themselves take up new impulses while unconscious during sleep; and we are also unconscious as far as the real 'I' is concerned during the day; yet morality must be planted into it. The human being is still a baby as regards morality, whereas intellectuality (based on the perfection of the long-existing physical and etheric bodies) can be developed in sleep. That is why moral progress is so difficult compared to intellectual development.[56] When we go to sleep, we leave behind our moral (and religious) feeling with the physical body, and our soul and spirit live in the etheric body with the moral purposes of the higher spirits as an a-moral being.

What the ego and the astral body do take with them into sleep is *moral responsibility*; they present to the spiritual entities all the inner morality they developed during the day, and are compelled now to let the world of soul and spirit work on what they have brought. Having had a moral impulse, or done a moral deed, our ego and astral body must be taken up by beings of the Third Hierarchy according to cosmic spiritual law. But if we have done an immoral deed or had an immoral impulse, we cannot enter their realm with the residue it has formed in us; what is immoral is rejected and thrust back into the bodily nature. Thus in deep sleep we experience unconsciously the part of the spiritual aspect of our daily life of which we were quite unaware, we experience what the Gods think about our deeds and waking thoughts. We are good or bad according to our nearness to the Gods, which thus depends also on our previous lives.

In surrendering in deep sleep to the universally extraspatial world which overcomes time, we reach the lawfulness of the world spirit. When all egoism is overcome, elements of the true supersensible love can be added. Only here do we recognise the entire, self-contained human being as he is eternal. In the simple varying intensities of warmth there is in reality a world-permeating morality, in which the human being develops.[57]

The will-related *ego* thus meets the entities of the *spiritual* world in sleep and is given spiritual form, depending entirely on its moral constitution – a kind of furrowing, like the surface of the brain. We depend on sleep for everything we have of inner moral attitude. Everything evil in our soul makes the ego waste away, everything good allows it to develop freely.

The feeling-related *astral* body makes direct contact with the *astral* world, where it is not formed but coloured, given tone, taste, and imbued with power from that world – all this whirls and twirls together within it. This kind of inward experience is extremely mobile, glittering and gleaming, shifting and changing, growing luminous and fading away again. The powers that bring this about derive from the being of limbs and metabolism, working from below. In response to the question that we put on falling asleep regarding our moral constitution, we are all the time in dialogue with entities of the spiritual world, who give a furrowing and a colouring to our soul that tell us the true state of our inner being.[58]

While we sleep our moral qualities are thus revealed by the individual colouring of the streams of light which flow in through our head into the inner parts of the body. In the immoral person these are brownish-red or reddish-brown, in a person of high moral deeds they are lilac-violet. On falling asleep or waking there is a struggle around the pineal gland between these streams and those of the intellectual element of the etheric body streaming upwards as movements of light from the region of the heart. This struggle may be violent or, in the case of moral pre-eminence, a peaceful glow of glimmering light is seen round the pineal gland, often extending down to the heart. We in fact produce within ourselves a second man from our moral or immoral life, who goes with us through death.

Moral consciousness depends by day on life in the etheric body which is derived not only from the four ethers but also from the moral essence of the cosmic ether. This is, however, present only in the neighbourhood of stars and planets, as well as on the earth. Between the stars it is driven out by the action of sunlight (not by the sun itself, which contains the very source and origin of moral ether), and Ahriman has access to it; as father of lies he makes the good appear bad and the bad appear good. That is why the bad person has no pangs of conscience and sleeps well, whereas the highly conscientious person, whose moral sensitivity has entered deeply into his soul, may feel guilty, and sleeps badly. The enticement in sleep to evil is indeed great, and one can easily bring back terrible demonic forces of temptation, until back in the body one feels the voice of conscience. These forces of temptation merge by day into the moral powers that live in the etheric body. Today it behoves us to arm ourselves against these forces, because with our increasingly strong ego-consciousness we are no longer protected by the group-soul feeling.[59]

Because during sleep we are freed from all laws of nature, we can as free beings act on *moral impulses grasped in pure thinking* (see *Philosophy of Freedom*). Since our thoughts themselves are only images, which cannot compel us, we can insert our night being, which has become independent during sleep, into our pure thoughts and act on them as free beings. As such, moral impulses can only be applied to waking life. The forces of the moral-etheric aura pour through the head by day to encounter the ego in the blood, but in sleep the ego has withdrawn from the head. Thus morality involves a direct influence of our spiritual environment on the forces in the blood radiating from the ego throughout the entire human being. In order that moral impulses received through conscious thought can really attain to effective activity, we plunge in sleep down into the divine will, where divine forces transform our moral impulses into will forces. The impulses we thus receive are shadows from higher spiritland.

Exusiai, Dynamis and Kyriotetes bear what we grasp in our thoughts arising from sleep into our bodily nature as *moral power*; and Seraphin, Cherubim and Thrones bear this power out into the world, so that our own moral forces become world-creative powers, providing a proper basis for Jupiter evolution.*
We could experience that moral order if, with Christ's help, we worked our way into the peace of the fixed stars, seen in the form of their counterparts or copies within us. Only a small part, however, of the moral impression gained in sleep comes through as *conscience*, because on waking the physical body conceals it.

* The next stage of Earth evolution, the 'new Jerusalem' (Rev 21).

Our aberrations, often entirely hostile to the world, arise from the moral sphere as if from unfathomable depths of the will, as do all pricks of conscience and self-reproach.

It should be widely known that when we utter – or even only think – a lie, it causes a devastating kind of explosion in the astral world. Even mere colouring of truth cumulatively hardens part of the physical body at night, and parts of the higher Beings who descend become detached as phantoms. If the etheric body is harmed by bad laws or social measures, the bad feelings arising bring about detachments working as spectres or ghosts. And when someone overrules another by unjustified advice, enclosures of the astral body are at night detached as demons, spirits of prejudice. All these whiz and whirr through our life.[60] A lie which is conscious lives while we sleep in spaceless, timeless eternal being, where everything is made ready to correct it. But if it is in the unconscious it remains with the body, and works for the destruction of the cosmos, and above all for the destruction of humanity itself. Man can escape this only by striving after inner truth as regards the supreme questions of existence.

The whole human moral element is brought back by the ego and astral body when we wake, which the physical and etheric bodies then soak up. The effects are seen in the way we behave, and in the way the life of the internal organs is tuned. The whole significance of sleep lies essentially in the moral structure of our inner nature.[61] But the ego and astral body cannot in any way take hold of the physical body in any moral sense; we bring back wisdom , but only acquire morality in the physical world.

18. Sleepwalking

We do not normally walk in our sleep because the ego is not then within the physical body. Sleepwalkers are quite distinct from ordinary human beings, both in their life on earth and in their pre-earthly life, where they were hostile to anything spiritual. When they take on their physical body, there remains an affinity with the moon forces, and they pay less heed to their body. As a result they cannot satisfactorily unite their astral bodies with the physical.

In our etheric body we are subject not to the earth forces but to the moon forces; and in sleepwalkers these are temporarily active. When, through an instinctive destiny, earthly gravity is withdrawn, the moon forces can begin to act as counter-gravity, and the sleeper starts to wander about in the moonstruck way of the somnambulist. Influences we receive during sleep are similar to those of the lunar phases, not as a direct influence but as an inner rhythm, pointing to a common origin in earlier earth conditions.

In deep sleep Saturn forces have a slight effect upon everyone, influencing the soul; but under special circumstances these forces, by means of the consciousness soul, may lead the person who cannot withstand their effects into robotic action as a sleepwalker or a sleeptalker.* One can observe a transition to actual activity from a single perception to intention, compulsive automatic action or words.

The consciousness of the sleepwalker is spread over the whole life of the environment, and goes over into other beings around him. A person whose ego is not properly in the astral

---

* Sleeptalking occurs in phase 2 of sleep, because the rhythmic system, not the brain or limbs, is affected.

body by day may in sleep have extraordinarily strong experiences, in fine detail, of the external world around him, for example, awareness of the delicate flavour of apples in his orchard. He also has pale thoughts, the after-effects in the astral body from waking life. The physician will call such a person psychologically disturbed, but the priest knows he can give genuine revelations from the spiritual world.

Although the ego has its physical expression in the blood circulation, and we experience its concept centred in the head, its activity is actually tethered to and held in check by the autonomic nervous system radiating as shaping force from the solar plexus. But when there is a break in the normality of these organs, the ego unites with the spiritual forces of the environment, leading to somnambulism or mental illness. Similarly, if the astral body is unleashed from the processes of the spinal nervous system, or the etheric body from the cerebral nervous system, somnambulism may occur.[62]

Somnambulism can arise without any trigger, or it may respond to what someone is saying or thinking. The person cannot control what he sees or does, and can fall prey to the most remarkable illusions. The Ahrimanic world has completely different concepts from our earthly world of good and evil; so when the somnambulist has experiences in that world, concepts of good and evil are shattered. The dreamless sleep consciousness of etheric and physical bodies, present also by day, even though ego and astral consciousness cannot descend to it, may itself manifest in somnambulistic actions, in response to influences experienced in a previous incarnation.

When in a somnambulistic state, we descend to a far deeper consciousness, and become dreamily cognisant of great cosmic laws more vividly than in our ordinary dreams. We experience the activities of the sympathetic nervous system, thus sensing the life of the entire cosmos. At such times the sleep-walker senses his ancestors within himself – they are audible in his blood – and he duly partakes in their remote life.

19. The Forming of Karma

Sleep is actually the window through which we look at karma, become familiar with it, and work at its future shaping. From the night, karma then gradually enters our life of day. When we are 'outside the body' in sleep, we are actually in our pre-earthly state, or have returned to our former lives on earth. Through Intuition we come to know the 'I' that bears this karma. Our willing, bound to limbs and metabolism, is completely immersed in sleep, even by day. Inherent in it, however, is the 'I' which existed throughout our former earth lives. That is where karma holds sway, only all the impulses working from the past are veiled in sleep, even during waking life.

As sleep progresses we begin to dive down into the experiences undergone in our previous earth life, then into those of the life before that, and so on backwards. We reach and pass our first, most distant life as an individual, and by the time awakening comes we reach the condition when we were not yet separate from the cosmos. Only then can we return again into our body. The same holds good for a short nap – even then we rush with tremendous, lightning-like rapidity through all our earthly lives. The whole of sleep is a unity, and the astral body is an unconscious prophet, it surveys the whole of sleep up to the point of waking; though in a nap what is remote may lack clarity, and not reach to where individual lives begin. Think of it: the whole of earth evolution, together with what the sleeper has experienced in previous lives! Karma is perpetually present, inscribed as it were into the World Chronicle; and every time we fall asleep we have the opportunity to approach this karma of ours. This is one of the great secrets of existence.[63] Our soul holds within itself not only its sleep experiences, but all those experiences of world evolution described in Occult Science, from the original Sun to its daughter in the sky.

The moment that we begin to have around us in sleep the constellations as well as the movements of the planets, we behold our karma in depth through our 'sun eye' (p76). And through an organ lying even deeper, extending over and involving the entire human being, we gain a powerful and vivid experience of the mysteries of birth and death. Everything that we have had to do with one another as person to person, all human ties, either in some past earth life or in the present, show themselves to this spiritual eye. We feel that we stand indeed within the stream of our whole life-destiny.

Through Intuition we know why we have certain capacities, why we are connected with this or that personality, why this or that blow of destiny has befallen us. But we can learn to know our destiny only when we can penetrate into the inner being of the minerals. We live in this mineral world every night; but every time we have to awaken, the Christ force must again come to our aid – we could enter the crystal realm without it, but could not emerge again. This is connected with the Christ force itself (since the Mystery of Golgotha He has dwelt in our inner being), not with our belief in it.[64]

What comes pre-eminently before the soul's eye as experiences during sleep is newly forming destiny. When in sleep we can illuminate what lay in the will whilst awake, we come upon the karma working from previous lives; when we begin to penetrate the experiences whilst asleep, we see how karma weaves out of our free actions what will be first realised in the next life. In the consciousness of deep sleep an actual and real nexus of forces weaves, lives and is spun, together with divine spirits. This leads us after waking into connection with the working out of our karma.

During sleep we project into the purely spiritual world a whole sum of impulses which we would otherwise press into actions, and they pass over with us beyond death. Our future karma is that which would like to become deed but does not. It is experienced between willing and deed. All that we bear within us as moral impulses is always there; and in perceiving it we learn to know ourself in so far as we have made ourself during life. Every morning on awaking we pass through the region of thoughts which is our past karma, every evening we pass into our future karma.[65] We in fact produce within ourselves a second man from our moral or immoral life, which goes with us through death. We carry the result of our karma into the physical body during sleep, but that has no organ to perceive it. We ought only to see karma with organs of spiritual Intuition.

The real nature of soul and spirit in sleep is seen to come from the limbs and metabolism. During sleep the ego works upon the moral impulses we have absorbed in preparation for our next life on earth; they clothe themselves in our moral disposition, in our temperament and trend of character – all wrongly attributed to heredity. We in fact put into the world an image of the moral constitution from the present life which will be embodied in the head in the next life. Whilst asleep we unconsciously experience too the forces of the future which the unborn child consciously encounters prior to conception. Out of these forces come the impulse to heal and promote the interests of civilisation.

See also section 28.

VI   REVERSION TO FIRST PHASE

20. Bodily Restorative Processes

The restoration in sleep of the damage caused daily by ordinary
life to the physical body is a complex and wonderful process,
especially because each region of the body has its own particular
function.

The fundamental situation is that the physical body
always tends to disintegrate and decay (as it does at death). This
is prevented and restored by the etheric formative forces of nourishment and growth, which are of four kinds – warmth, light,
sound/chemical and life itself. These are in continual flow, but
need to be given specific form. Form is provided by the astral
body in accordance with the human archetype, which is of
cosmic origin. Therefore the astral body needs to leave the physical and etheric bodies in sleep to refresh its cosmic impulse. This
is sustained by the real or cosmic 'I', but modified by the heredity,
environment, and destiny of each individual ego. The same
activity is carried out by everyone, and without it one cannot
arrive at the secret of sleep.

We saw (p55) how in first phase sleep, when the ego and
astral body are in the elementary kingdoms of nature, the
sunlight preserved within them, together with the changing
moon forces, prevents further deterioration. But only from being
actually within the worlds of soul and spirit, of planets and fixed
stars, can the astral body draw forth the health-giving forces, so

that progress to second and third phase sleep is necessary (fig.1). Meanwhile the lower parts of the astral and ego auras unite more closely with the physical and etheric bodies than by day, and project downward into the earth (fig.2). These auras which work from below depend upon the upper aura developing sufficient forces from the world of stars to attract and stimulate them.

After about an hour and a half asleep, due to an innate rhythm, the upper astral aura reverts to the first phase environment nearby, but is now charged with the harmonies and patterns of its cosmic home. The lower aura withdraws similarly. We must next ask how these are brought into conjunction with the etheric body, still in bed, to restore the physical.

Consider first the head, and specifically the brain. Our ordinary intellectual thinking – not the universal thoughts or sense-free spiritual thinking – causes mineral sedimentation, and these deposits have first to be dissolved (p81). Then the upper astral body, having just come back from the realm of the fixed stars, has within it subtle fleeting images, inverted replicas, of the whole cosmos – the objective world thoughts; and the lower astral body, with images from the interior of the earth bearing form principles from previous lives, works upwards. These are the creative forces which in infancy together formed the brain, and are later used to form our conscious images and sensations. In sleep, withdrawn from consciousness, they can again restore form to the brain objectively. (A spiritual researcher may notice just before waking a sequence of strange pictures felt to be in motion, like living beings related to one another.) Then the instreaming forces of light ether (p57) can combine with these pictures of what is sound and healthy, and begin to unite them with the physical brain, reconstructing the element worn down by day like a craftsman working with his tools, so that the nerves are rebuilt robustly. However, the forces of light ether affect only nerves, not muscles.

Consider now the rhythmic processes of heart and lung, which never cease throughout life. But the personal interests, the sympathies and antipathies which we bring to outer objects, the stresses of daily hopes and fears, the excesses of our turbulent emotions or the cold lack of empathy and love, all tend to distort their rhythms, which constantly need to be restored and reinvigorated. These rhythms of pulse and breath exist only in time, and therefore require different treatment. Our inner being – sentient, rational and spiritual souls – consequently draws down the rhythms and harmonies from the music of the spheres, the cosmic rhythms resulting from the relative movements of the planets, according to the relationships made with them during second phase sleep (p69). These can then be united with the etheric forces of sound ether (chemical ether) – the only carriers of this music– which are borne in with the inhaled air (p57), so that they permeate and refresh the architectural forces of space – not the substances – for the physical heart and lungs. We thus tremble and pulsate nightly in response to these harmonies, bringing order into that which by day we had brought into disorder.

Processes of the metabolic-limb system are continually asleep – we are never conscious of how we digest or move. However, the soul and bodily impairment incurred during the day needs to be restored. So during phase three sleep the astral body draws down the necessary images and form principles from the whole spiritual cosmos beyond the sun. These then work downwards from the head, through the nervous system, to fill the lower organism – where the lower ego and astral body are intensely active (p46) – with marvellous thoughts. Powers of the eye closed in sleep, for example, imbue the kidney system with cosmic images, and other organs in the head imprint different aspects of the cosmos similarly. Moral principles and impulses work into them, but indirectly (p86). These images and principles then unite with the forces of life ether, which were inhaled with the sound ether and, as inhalation passes to exhalation, are alone carried further to the metabolic-limb system. The true nature of the will thus awakens unconsciously, permeates our organism, and invigorates it, restoring both the organs and their organic functions. But if this rises to consciousness it becomes thoroughly evil. As Genesis says (3:22), we are not to see the forces of life, of restoration.

Meanwhile the real or cosmic 'I', meaning the Beings of the Higher Hierarchies and even the Trinity (p79), which is tethered to the solar plexus, works in connection with the autonomic system in the warmth process connected with past lives (p82), and with the formation of the blood. The intermediary here may be the moral ether (p86). These marvellous processes of will, working from above downwards as in a true fiery element, are governed by a level of consciousness of spirit man, although in our inner life there is but a faint recollection of their mighty cosmic life. We are thus created anew out of the spirit every night.

As the astral impulses from the upper astral aura pass through the head to the lower astral aura, they also kindle there the sound and life ethers sufficiently to cause some periodic twitching of the muscles of the face, including intermittent flickering of the eyes – the rapid eye movements (REMs). After a short time of REM sleep the astral body returns to its cosmic home. This whole process is repeated, on average four times per night for adults. As the night progresses the episodes of non-REM sleep become shorter and those of REM sleep longer. The REM process always precedes waking, when dreams are experienced, and may lead to sporadic waking. The upbuilding forces from the spiritual cosmos brought down into the body are obviously of particular importance during REM sleep; and in the development of the infant and young child REM sleep is consequently much more frequent, especially at sleep onset. In this context rapid eye movements indicate that bodily restorative processes are taking place, but they do not play a significant part.

What is made good by night is destroyed again the next day, and there is always a small surplus of destructive force. This surplus gradually collects, as a result of which the natural death of old age ensues. Sleep thus unfolds healing forces of a special kind, but fundamentally can repair only what we have used up within the limits of the spiritual predisposition brought through birth; whereas spiritual science opens a higher source of healing.[66] (R.G.S.)

VII WAKING UP

21. The Approach

The moment the body no longer bears the after-influences of the astral body and ego within it we have to wake up, or the body would disintegrate. The astral body is connected to the physical by a sort of band of substance, part of the etheric body. During sleep there is a shining stripe, which gets thinner as the astral body goes further away. In some places it is brighter and thicker than in others, and these are the places that lead the astral body back to the physical body. A yearning, an impulse to return to the physical body, darkens the brightness of the spiritual world; to the clairvoyant, bright rays expressing the yearning proceed from the soul to the body. In the morning the soul, being close to but still outside the body, notices from the condition of the skin that the body has been restored and craves to be in it again. Awaking occurs in a single moment. We wake up when we are in sympathy with the body again, and slip into all the individual organs, which are now refreshed. The process is such that in all essentials the astral body penetrates the etheric body and the ego penetrates the physical body; but of course all principles interpenetrate.

We should never return to the body if we truly knew the spiritual world and had grown to be part of it, but we have the unconscious wish to return to the physical world. We feel that we shall not be spiritually empty when we wake, for we bring down the Spirit dwelling in our soul: Per Spiritum Sanctum

Reviviscimus. What can truly be called the Trinity thus successively permeates our spiritual life in sleep.

The astral body knows how long we shall sleep. It returns with the resonances from the harmony of the spheres. Thus on waking we pass again through the element of music in spiritland – we may perceive whether the sentient body (in the minor) or the sentient soul (in the major) is the stronger. It is the force that drives Mars, working in the sentient soul, that brings the soul back on waking. It is often difficult to draw back the astral body, there are hindrances, spiritual storms and percussions perceptible to Inspiration. This is due to an irregularity in the working of the Saturn forces, which connect especially to the physical upper man.

Having during sleep lived the day backwards to the previous morning, the astral body now jerks the inner soul life quickly forwards again; and it is this which condenses the astral impressions* within it into enduring etheric memory pictures. We cultivate this power of memory together with the Archangels.[67] Only because of the intervals of sleep is memory so dimmed that we can endure it in ordinary consciousness.

As the astral body and ego return, they encounter first the etheric body. It is this encounter with the memory-thought tissue that gives rise to dreams, which will be considered in later sections. The astral body, coloured according to its moral reactions, enters an ether body structured by the cosmos, and has to adapt to it. Moreover cosmic astral powers also influence human astral powers – for example, geometrical concepts which hold good for the cosmos influence earthly concepts. Every time we wake we have to make the effort to take possession of our body

* Short term memories

again rightly – it actually gets lost while we sleep. The etheric body tends to dissolve into four separate figures each night, one like an angel, others like a lion, an eagle, and a bull. Each morning the astral body has to exert itself to synthesize these four parts into something truly human.

After passing right through the etheric body, whilst between the etheric and physical bodies, but before entering the physical body, a whole world appears before the soul. As quickly as it arises, it fades again, and before we think to grasp it, it is gone. We must cultivate great presence of mind to experience this thought-weaving of cosmic thoughts[68] (p52). We thus wake up not from darkness but out of an ocean of thoughts, the super-logical cosmic thought world that we are too weak to retain. This is distinct from our daily thoughts (which draw it down), but very similar to thought-flashes or moral intuition. Only medi-tative thinking reveals that we waken out of this ocean of thoughts, a spiritual world which we cannot bring into the body as shadow thoughts, for it lies behind the memory mirror.

The etheric body and physical body are thus caught up in continual thought activity while we are asleep, although we are outside this activity. (The etheric body thinks less well when in normal consciousness we are within it!) As we awaken we meet the thinking that has gone on while we slept, and each morning we awaken changed. At the instant of waking the spir-itual researcher has a direct experience of feeling himself as inde-pendent of his own thinking. The images of this cosmic thinking activity prior to awakening begin to unite with the brain, enabling one to go further with one's own thinking. No one who has not really grasped in observation the moment of waking can truly grasp what it means to say 'I think'.

Only what has been experienced outside the body by the astral organisation can be brought back into the thoughts of the etheric body, not what is experienced there by the ego, which remains subconscious even for Imagination. We thus lack today the power to deal with the wishes and desires experienced by the ego in connection with earthly affairs that are gone over during sleep.

What we do bring back from the cosmos is the will. Part of the will-system returns through the inter-twirling thoughts of the head that form an undercurrent of our ordinary consciousness, but can only day-dream while we are awake. This descending will first transforms subconsciously the chaotic thought-tissue of dreams into orderly memories. We become aware how it then makes the interweaving pictures into fantasy, the inventive faculty – a dreamy person simply gives himself up to the surging of arbitrary thought. Lastly, the will brings order based on the cosmic logic of our inner organs, so that we judge and form conclusions accordingly, especially those of mathematics. (If we did not form logical thought by our will it would be compulsive thought.) This descending will finally encounters, by means of the rhythms of breathing and pulse, the other will* rising from the body, and becomes outer activity.[69]

We also bring back in form and colour answers to the unconscious questions which we put on going to sleep concerning our moral constitution – they are transformed in waking life into the voice of conscience. The causes of many illnesses also lie in these answers, for our physical and etheric organs have to deal fully with everything that our ego and astral body bring back with them from the world of spirit.

* Instinct, impulse

Within 24 hours we pass in a microcosmic sense through the course of the year. By day the ego and astral body begin to graze and demolish the growing blossoming life which has sprung up during the night – the physical/etheric of body-summer and the withdrawn ego/astral of spirit-winter are replaced by body-winter and spirit-summer. Thus there is an intermingling in us of conditions which in nature work in sequence; in us they neutralise each other, and it is this that enables us to become free beings.[70] As the moment of waking approaches, the summer-like condition in the physical and etheric bodies is brought to a close and clear day consciousness lights up.

The ahrimanic element carries us, quite properly, from sleeping to waking. When too little of the luciferic impulse is carried into waking, the ahrimanic element presses us down too strongly; we are pushed down into the realm of emotions and passions, submerged in the life of animal instinct. And the ego is made to enter too thoroughly into the bodily aspect, preventing us from remaining in the realm of good and evil, of moral impulses. Conversely, when the luciferic impulse works in an unjustified way, dreams rise up and work back into waking life, pushing us into an unhealthy kind of mysticism.

22. Return to the Body

The fully awakened *ego* enters the body, but *not its physical processes* – it enters the world of pictures created at the innermost level of the body by external processes; and in this way the 'I' is given thinking cognition. In feeling the ego permeates the real physical body, not just the pictures, but only in a dreamy state; otherwise the soul would burn up, being unable to endure what occurs in the body as feeling. What happens in willing we experience only in sleep.[71]

The ego approaches from all sides, from the Beings and realities of the worlds, and on waking it is always present in its substantiality as a kind of ego-light-aura around the body. But it is not to be sought at any particular spot. The forces which are let through build up the physical organism of the senses; what is not let through is the content of our sensations. Thus it is not that on waking the ego and astral slip right into us and are then completely in the body – they remain united with the whole spiritual environment; we need only imagine our relation to the air to get the picture, except that when we breathe out again the air disperses, whilst ego and astral retain their form during sleep and return to the body.

There is no such thing as matter, only forces; and our ego is connected while awake with earth, water, air elements and part of the warmth. The ego slips in only to the extent that the physical body loses its weight – it enters into direct connection with the gravity of the earth, shutting the physical body out of the process. Similarly we slip with our ego-organisation directly into the fluid organisation, into the forces of buoyancy of the etheric body – for example, our brain swims in the cerebro-spinal fluid, and our ego is directly within the buoyancy.[72]

From outside we pass too across the surface of our body, through the eyes and the optic nerves, working from a kind of 'beyond', juggling with the pictures around us as we slip through. Then we come into close connection with the nerves that now make the pictures into an orderly world. On fully entering the physical body we turn round, as it were, look out through our eyes and see things rightly; and similarly with all the other senses.

The *upper astral body* spreads out along the paths of the moving breath, and the part of it that is active in the senses contacts the delicate ramifications of the breathing process, penetrating into its subtle rhythms. This meeting of the air with the senses is the essential factor in all sensory processes, where the Angels work and weave. And as breath-beings we have roots in the world of the Archangels, who pass in and out as we go to sleep and awaken. Inspiration perceives how reflections on the soul of the planetary movements continue in awakeness as a stimulant to the rhythms of breathing and blood circulation. We owe it to this that our breathing and circulatory processes are 'enfired'.

But if at the moment of waking the dream-quality of ideation were permeated only by the life of the senses, we should come only to concepts resembling fantasy pictures. Something else is given by the outer world which we find in the process of fertilisation – it is the male element of life itself that now gives concepts their clearly defined form.[73]

Diagram 3

The *astral body** with the ego enclosed within it, first re-enters the *physical* body through the tips of the fingers and toes. This statement must be taken literally. They really need the whole day to fill us as far as the head – after half an hour they will have reached the ankles and possibly the wrists, and at mid-day it is as if we sat in a hipbath. They are in perpetual flow. But they work spiritually through the whole bodily space even when they occupy only fingers and toes – indeed when only approaching, they can be felt throughout the body.[74]

After a good deep sleep we feel tired out. Thus sleep's healing power is only felt an hour or an hour and a half after waking, because immediately on waking, having worked on our organs during sleep, we are not yet in them enough to use them. We often notice on waking that something rises up from the physical body, namely the restorative forces; but if we are ill or have something diseased in our organism, that also ascends and works to expel the illness upwards, causing a certain moodiness and unhappiness. Only after an hour and a half can we say we are free of this.

Nevertheless, on waking the *lower parts* of the ego and astral auras (corresponding to the lower parts of the trunk), which during sleep have been more within than the upper parts and more closely united with the physical and etheric bodies, go forth again to some degree; only part of them remains within.[75] As soon as we take in the ego and astral body, the etheric body is displaced, pushed down from the head into the other elements of the organism, where it stays while we remain awake; on going to sleep it spreads back into the head, just as it is in the rest of the body.

* The astral body comes from the spaceless realm, it merely assumes the form of spatial activity.

On waking, the physical body says: the earth absorbed me during the night, it wants to make me into dust; I have only survived because in previous days you have, through your ego and astral body, held me together and the forces of coherence continue to work in me. The etheric body wants to disperse into the cosmos and now says: only because I have grown used to resembling you have I retained human form; actually the cosmic forces would have cast me to the winds whilst you were outside me, asleep. If we could bring our sleep experiences to consciousness we should want on waking to impress them on the physical and etheric bodies, to give ourselves every time a new face, because the one we have would remind us of our sins during former lives; but these bodies could not bear it.

The aftermath of everything experienced by night is carried over into the life of day. As the irreligious ages continue, human beings will carry over a state of soul-disintegration that will be a strong factor in depriving the organism of the forces for the proper distribution of ingested food, leading to ominous illness. To be healthy we need to carry over a feeling of belonging to the divine spiritual beings into whose activities our eternal core of being sinks during sleep.

Especially in the ailing, waking up may bring a slightly unhealthy feeling of oppression, the need to lift oneself out of certain depths in the course of the day. This may intensify to a stupefied head, an element of heaviness. It is due to a very first glimpse of present karma borne from past lives. A very burdensome karma radiates unhealthy deposits into the head, whereas a good karma radiates health-giving deposits. With important events about to happen, of which we are unconsciously aware, we do not wake up as we ordinarily do, but we do not notice it.[76]

The part of the physical body relating to the ego acts during sleep like salt, whereas the part relating to the astral body (the astral-physical element) exercises mercurial powers. When the ego and astral body return on waking, they enter the salty/mineral and the mercurial/vitalising principles of the body respectively; they fill them with what they have gained in the spiritual world, influencing the highly developed physical body – the instrument of the intellect. This mineralising process is especially strong at the moment of waking.

As we pass into the different organs, we also slip into the very outermost ramifications of the sensory nerves; throughout the day we are there, touching the nerve-endings all the time. We are not normally conscious of this, but one who consciously experiences the moment of waking feels as if he were being pricked all over. What do we do with these pricks if they do not reach our consciousness? We project them into space, and they are then the atoms: that in truth is the origin of atomism. As with a reflecting mirror, we conceive that the whole of space is filled with what in fact we project into it.[77]

When we connect with the earthly element as we wake, we may experience tones, for every solid has sounds in it; if really attentive we may experience as if someone were knocking at the door. This is related to the dead, who live in the solid material in the first days after death – tones arise when they abandon the earth. Soft sounds are easily heard, but if one hears all kinds of things, that is a danger and we must be cautious – it can only be spirit beings of a lower nature.

23. Awaking to Outer Life

The moment we wake, we pass as ego through the portal of our own being; but here stands the Lesser Guardian of the Threshold, who at once diverts us into the outer world, where we see only what beneficent Beings place before our vision. To pass him and enter consciously into our inmost self – into the physical, etheric and astral bodies – would give rise to the life of mysticism.

The essential fact on waking is that we view our body from without, not from within; our gaze is directed to the outer world. The veil that prevents us from beholding the spirituality underlying it is the sentient body, which is wholly concerned with the sense world. This is necessary because we could not endure the sight of the soul, but would feel a sense of shame of overpowering strength because of its imperfection compared to the perfection of the body. The spiritual being who every morning stands before us, and protects us while we are still immature from sight of our own inner self, is the Lesser Guardian of the Threshold. He protects us from the sight of the destructive activity of our desires, urges and passions, whilst the Greater Guardian protects us from penetrating to the macrocosmic forces standing behind nature.[78]

Things of nature tell us the truth about themselves because during sleep we have appreciated them through our soul's presence with all that is spiritual in them. In sleep we have then accurately experienced inwardly something external to us. On waking we retain the inclination and affinity towards nature, and recognise it as an outer world. This relationship gives us the earthly concept of truth.

Waking is a battle of the single lonely soul, which has justifiable feelings of helplessness and inadequacy in the face of the giant powers of nature; this daily battle affects the very essence and individual character of our being. Waking scares away the good elemental beings, messengers of the Second Hierarchy, who are continually working on our being in the spiritual world; and Ahriman covers them with his sense pictures, while Lucifer fills our soul with so much pride and delusion that we receive false ideas of the spiritual world.

If with ordinary consciousness we were always aware during sleep, people of a more Ahrimanic disposition would go about by day as if their consciousness had suffered a kind of paralysis; while those of a more Luciferic disposition would be in a state of confusion, with their thoughts and feelings in a perpetual jumble. Before we dare tread on the side of the Creator, we must have come to love the creation. Otherwise we should come back each morning with a terrible hatred of the sense world, and the impulse to destroy it.

When we have once again united all the parts of our being, it is then the sun that summons us out into ordinary life. Nor is it merely a picture but a deep truth to say that the sun recalls the astral body and ego together with the three souls into the physical body.

Impulses received during the night influence our life of day, and we can reach no reasonable decisions if they have not first been experienced in advance. During the night we go through prophetically (although unconsciously) what we shall encounter next day. Then when we cultivate thoughts already experienced and prepared during the preceding night, they rise again and the decisions we make will be fruitful. We look at the events of the coming day, but without always carrying over that vision into day consciousness – it is our Angel who has the clear consciousness. We should be filled with the conviction that we ought to make real in a fruitful way what we have arranged in cooperation with our Angel – if people had felt this, how different events would be! Thoughts not grasped at night but fetched out of the day's events will only lead us into misery.[79]

When by day the physical and etheric bodies impressed the essence of their activity on the astral body and ego, these resisted but had to adapt. What they have received continues vibrating during sleep, bringing back this echoed experience into the body next morning. Eurythmy brings back a wonderfully health-giving power to the body, singing does something similar to the whole system of movement, a physics experiment recollected brings pictures leading to underlying laws, and so on. In the night what is taught to a child works on within him – a true understanding of the whole human being is required, and if we leave out consideration of the night we make, for example, a child whose faculty of judgment is overstrained into a child of routine. During sleep we are not only physically rejuvenated, but we also bring back the arts from the higher worlds.

After all personal desires and opinions have been eliminated, and symbolic pictures experienced in deep meditation for a considerable period, it is first at the moment of waking that, turning attention away from everyday experience, real experiences of the spiritual world with some degree of vision become possible. We may become aware on waking of something wonderful, a quite tender feeling, an experience in the spiritual world which we cannot express in words. Forms develop in the colours that rise before us of something quite other than what we are used to seeing, although they must not then be taken for spiritual experiences. When we wake we should never at once have banal egoistic thoughts, which cut us off from the spiritual beings and forces in which we were plunged during sleep. We should first devote ourselves in self-forgetfulness to meditation as a holy duty, or at least link our first thoughts to those high Beings.

The moment of waking should thus be holy, because one should sense: I have come from the spiritual world, and everything good, everything that enables me to be a reasonable person, I have got to know through communion with the spiritual world, and with the dead, whilst asleep. However, if a person drowsy with sleep meditates but does not rise clearly enough into thoughts, he creates a powerful substance of desires around himself in which retrograde egotistical beings incarnate into his thought forms. The esotericist should say on waking: I come from whence I tarried before my body was created; and in meditation linger a few moments in this, kindling the holy fire one needs. Through prayer on waking we gain force from the spiritual world for daily life.

Various meditations for morning and evening have been given by Rudolf Steiner.[80]

Waking from Sleep

Sphere of Wisdom

O Ye![a] from spheres of light stream through this head,
Move there in ways which spirits pure are led,
Damp well down his brain's insane confusion,[b]
From his striving untangle all doubt's fire and fear
To guide him within from pathways of illusion.[c]

In daily experience four goals are clear;
Now lead him on, untouched by apprehension:

— First strive for countenance that fills with light,
— Then spirit's quest for power hold fast.
— Once lame-wing'd senses move again in flight,
His day in freedom can unfold
— Thus truest spirit duty it fulfils:
Through holy light to lead him where he wills.

---

[a] elemental beings from the Sphere of Wisdom
[b] with ordered thought
[c] the illusion of dreams

Aesthetic Sphere

O Ye![d] surround the head with airy circling,
Your paths in noble elfin fashion tracing,
And soften in the heart its harvest grim,
Remove reproach's bitter, glowing arrows,[e]
Within him make all pure from horror's gleam.

Four in number are the nightly hollows,
Now, friendly, fill them up without a seam:

  — First lower head down on the pillow cool,
  — Bathe it then in dews from Lethe's flood released;
  — Soon limbs, cramp-stiffened, will again grow supple,
In rest, against the day his strength's increased.
  — Fulfil most comely duty of the elf,
Return to holy light man's self.

[d] elemental beings of myths and sagas
[e] conscience, pleasure and displeasure

Moral Sphere

O Ye![f] stream through this head with strength to move,[g]
And in good earthly deeds yourselves soon prove.
So boldly stamp out torment of absurdity,[h]
Ennoble desire's power, wherein dark forces surge,
Abduct his soul, away from spirit-fatality.

In human obsession, pathways four do merge,
Tear them away from embrace of infirmity:

– Conquer the fires in which the senses groan,
– Illumine that which dies in pleasure,
– And hear how speak in ensouled tone
The powers that match eternal measure.[i]
– Attempt to strive in world-willed action,
Awaken him to life-benediction.

Rudolf Steiner
from 'The Riddle of Humanity' 6.8.16 (5)
tr. J.F.Logan

[f] spirit beings from the astral sphere
[g] in deeds
[h] desires and passions
[i] deeds of destiny

VIII   DREAMS

24. Introduction

We have seen that in sleep the astral body and ego separate from the physical and etheric bodies. Dreams enter consciousness when the astral body first regains contact with the etheric or whilst it severs contact, in both cases completely separated from the physical. The etheric body is then able to receive impressions of what goes on in the astral body and ego, without interference from the physical body and its sense impressions.

We can distinguish two main kinds of dream. They may point to the life of our inner organs, transformed by the astral body into symbolic pictures (sec.25). Or else they may be transformations of the experiences of the ego in the external world, either immediate or remote; here it is the dramatic sequence, the whole complex of feelings that is important (sec.26). In either case they can only be expressed by the etheric body in terms of mental pictures retained from everyday life. Different experiences may be expressed in the same dream, or the same experience may cause different dreams in different people. If the union of astral, etheric and physical bodies is regular, there is not an excess of dreams; but the moment the astral can dominate because the etheric is weakened, many and lively dreams occur.

Dreams are actually present both in ordinary consciousness and during sleep, but clothe themselves in pictures only on awakening or falling asleep. We in fact dream continuously, but whilst we are awake we overpower the dream with thinking consciousness. Though we speak of dreamless sleep, sleepers too are always dreaming, though so faintly as to be unnoticed. But we only have conscious dreams on going to sleep and waking. The forces of Jupiter drive the pictures of dreaming into the intellectual soul.

To dream *as we fall asleep* may mean that because of some irregularity, we do not immediately quit the etheric body. The day experiences, as they continue to resound, come in contact with the surrounding spiritual world, and there arises a chaotic, confused interplay which becomes the dream. Our conceptual life, which by its very nature wearies us, is not continued in our dreams. It is the emotions that appear in dream pictures. The will is seen to awaken at the moment when thinking falls asleep; it slips into the pictures perceived in the world of imaginative representations, and awakens them. The pictures are then woven out of will.

The *waking* dream may have quite a dramatic content, clothed in a certain fantasy which when awake we might have thought out quite differently. We see colours, movements etc, but hovering freely in space. Ideas are there too, even ideas of cause and effect. But coming from outside instead of being within, we cannot get near in the proper way to seize hold of our thinking quickly enough, for everything is the other way round; sense impressions arise before we can grasp them. That is why dreams reveal such curious logic. Feeling is the same condition as dreaming, a waking dream; it is the dream that rises out of the sleeping will and stimulates ideas.[81] On waking it is as if a dense wave flowed into one less dense; astral body and ego do not at once understand the thoughts that have continued all night in the etheric, they get confused, and there is a blockage which is the morning dream. When dreaming we live in a world comparable to that where interactions, normally invisible, occur between blossoming plants and sunlight. If we could half-waken from dream, we should experience around us the elementary world in which our soul has lived since the beginning of sleep. Actually this is impossible, but part of it reaches us in chaotic pictures.

Dreams are momentary, but they have their own inner time, which we ourselves extend on waking. In this way we transpose time into a dream. The dream itself has time reversed and does not conform to the circumstances of the ordinary world – the final event is usually the key to which the dream invents a fictitious cause. It is a creator in time. We cannot really see into our experiences before the moment of waking, we see only what induces us at that moment to insert symbolic pictures borrowed from daily life. The usual conscious experience is in fact a reminiscence, after the dream has departed.

Dreams are in reality misleading rather than enlightening. The dream world can help very little towards knowledge of the soul life until we have knowledge about sleep from other means. The quality of experience of a dream differs according to what lives in the soul; for example, a person with a bad conscience or a worry will have very different dreams from one who can yield himself to the peace and blessedness of the spiritual world. However, the dream shows us very clearly the independence of soul life from the outer life of the body, and to a more conscious and delicate observation appears as a kind of awakening to the life of the spirit (sec.27).

We are released in dreams from the laws that bind us to sense perception and logic, yet we seem to divine in them mysterious laws of their own, fascinating and alluring, which we tend to compare with the play of fancy and creative imagination. Their arbitrary, nonsensical character comes about because the astral body, disconnected from the physical organs, cannot relate to 'proper' objects and events of the outer world. Ordinary logic is silenced; when a dream appears logical, that is because we have incorporated a memory of logical sequence into it. Or, if we seem to find a solution to a problem, it could be the release of tension by the dream that enables us to do so.

Dreams are sometimes haunted by knowing, through the night's experience of the astral body, what a dreadful fellow one really is. Things can be quite immoral there, the criteria of morality are not applicable. We may do the strangest things that would normally cause terrible pangs of conscience, without conscience stirring at all. For dreams are a remnant of an earlier clairvoyant consciousness, before astonishment and conscience arose in ancient Greece. Moral judgment is thus silenced, we can do all kinds of misdeeds of which we would be ashamed in life. Writers on Shakespeare speak of dreams that carry moral reproaches, but it is actually a certain mood of satisfaction that we can morally say yes to something, rather than moral judgment; we must go to work much more exactly and intimately in seeking truth than is usual.

Dream consciousness is in fact a relic of the picture-consciousness of the Old Moon, and of long former periods of Earth evolution; yet it is essentially different in that it is transmuted by the presence of the ego. The dreamer in us is the man of Old Moon as he is in us today. We do many things half-aware, in which he directs or guides our thoughts, giving them a particular nuance of feeling.

Something is always living in our soul behind the dream picture, but the picture is a still greater illusion than the external world confronting us when awake. We must expect the actual objective occurrence to be veiled in accordance with the dreamer's degree of understanding. The dreamer lives in his own world of dream pictures; and as he does so he frequently finds it a good deal more vivid and gripping than everyday waking experience! But he experiences it in complete isolation, it is purely personal.

Dream-life has the greatest imaginable significance for a deeper knowledge of both world and man because it is a chink through which other worlds, either below or above the normal, shine into this one. But the great difficulty is to distinguish the sheer illusion from the reality behind it. The realm of dreams is one of those secrets in which very much is to be found, but which also attracts charlatans and superstition, so that special care is needed. Anyone concerned only with dream content is barking up the wrong tree, because this is no longer valid.

25. In Relation to the Body

Dreams are not experienced in the body, but arise as the soul makes contact with our bodily nature. They are really an expression of the soul-spiritual individuality; but what is actually experienced in the dream is not the eternal but the transitory, the normal content of life. Dreams may reflect a deeper experience of the body (which we also have in dreamless sleep). However, they are full of confusion because our ego and astral are not then inside the body, and it is the latter that puts our waking dreams aright; the relationship to the body is something we have to gain in another world.

Infant dreams show that the child has in him the powers to shape and develop his body, they are truly cosmic; he dreams of experiences before birth because these powers are still in him, and he needs them to develop his brain in fine detail. Dreams change in the course of life, and the wisdom we were given on descent is gradually changed into soul qualities.

In dreams the astral body shapes symbolic pictures of the inner organs, as by day the ego shapes pictures of external experiences. The former strongly resemble the earliest Imaginative experiences; but whereas Imaginations discern the pre-earthly being as a mighty etheric picture that crystallises into man's physical being, the dream gives rise to a caricature of an inner organ – although the caricature has the inherent possibility of growing into a perfect one.

The imprint of a memory on the etheric body is merely a sign, and has nothing to do with the actual experience. Strangely its shape resembles the head and part of the upper body including the hands. In dreams these homunculi, of which there are many thousands, arise in the etheric body, but leave a far weaker impress than do our daily recollections. This explains why the memory of dreams is so weak – no mark is left on the physical body.[82]

We must however study dreams very carefully if we are to see the weaving of the laws of our living organism, and the way external substances act within us, because the laws in the external world are no longer valid inside the skin. Whereas by day the etheric body is in regular inner movement in the whole body except the head, in sleep it begins to move within the head. In a waking dream we perceive the last movements of the etheric in the head – but this cannot happen if we wake up quickly.

If we can actually grasp the dream during the penetration of the etheric body by the astral, it feels mobile and substantial; with our ego we are within the picture in movement of soul, we plunge into our bodily nature in inner activity. What becomes of that which has thus been submerged in our body radiates back into our waking consciousness as feelings, emotions, passions – they are dreams submerged into our organisation. Feelings are as waves mounting from the day's dream life below the surface of conceptual life. The dream is formed to overcome certain tensions of soul. Often the feeling life is the decisive factor, the swinging between moods of anxiety and cheerfulness, tension and release, and so forth. The essential thing is the inner drama through which the soul passes, evoking feelings of joy or compulsion, but more often of anxiety, then greater anxiety, and lastly actual terror (p51). The pictures are only the clothing of the soul experience.

Irregularities in such rhythms as breathing or pulse may be perceived only in dreams. If the pictures of a waking dream are connected with conditions of fear, of vague dread (pleasure is less frequent) the cause will always be through a disorder in the breathing process. A dream of this kind recurring with absolute regularity is in fact always a symbolised reflection of what goes on in the body, and can often be connected with an oncoming illness. Something inside us is projected outwards for our perception, by which we are rent asunder – our unity of consciousness does not remain intact. We may then perceive whatever is painful or out of order. Such restless dreams, which are bad for health, interrupt the work of the astral body that produces new forces for the body.

Dreamers, particularly those who tend towards somnambulism, may see themselves with some illness, sometimes expressed in symbolic form, although actual symptoms may not appear until a few days later. A peculiar kind of instinct advises the fully fledged sleep-walker through a dream about his illness, and even about a particular remedy.

Dream life has a strange similarity to reflex action, in that neither results from reflection. As reflex actions are directed from the spinal cord, so there is inside the brain a mysterious spinal cord, invisible to external perception, which leads not to actions but to dream pictures and picture-actions. It reveals what the brain once was – an ancient spinal cord – but today it is only active when the brain in its new form is inactive. The dream is a relic of an old picture-consciousness that created myths and legends. But today it has lost its reality, its direct connection with the outside world. In the times of Ancient Egypt physicians dimmed the consciousness of their patient and induced a kind of hypnotic, dream-like sleep. They were able to control the soul-pictures that arose so that they acted on the body of the patient and healed him – no medicine was given.

Nightmares can be experienced if breathing becomes irregular and consciousness is forced back to an earlier stage prior to our present objective consciousness. The spirits of the air are unable to work into our blood and a host of lower spirits such as elves and sprites – appearing in the astral realm – have access to man. The physical expression of this is the nightmare, which is of course unhealthy.

We may experience nightmares as antipathy used to defend us against something that wants to invade us, reducing the experience of our egoity. Also the etheric body becomes too diffuse, bringing torment to the soul and enabling Lucifer to work. Every doubt, every problem, is a subtle form of nightmare; and whenever some doubt or question makes us uneasy, or when in a nightmare we feel a sensation of strangling, the breathing becomes more forceful, and must be harmonised.

During sleep the manner and method of nourishment also changes. A heavy meal just before sleep disturbs both the rhythmic system and the brain, and although we do not perceive the influence while we sleep, we experience the irregularity symbolically in dream pictures, and do not sleep well. The dream often represents the spiritual element in the body; if someone dreams of a tasty meal, the symbol of the meal may depict the real spiritual, astral content of the digestive organs.

In conditions of undernourishment and disturbed sleep, children may suffer from nightmares as a result of the inability of the astral body to interact rightly with the etheric body in the processes of digestion.

We are not aware that the processes which the chyme undergoes are perceived, tasted or felt by the liver, and thought by the kidneys. (The liver and kidneys have soul qualities and are able to perceive, just as we perceive with the sense organs in our head.) The chyme advances through the winding intestines and is permeated with trypsin which acts as a stimulus and can trigger dreams of snakes.[83] Or when we eat radishes such strong thoughts will come that they even produce powerful dreams. However, anyone who eats many potatoes will not have powerful thoughts but only dreams which will weigh him down; he will always be tired and want to sleep and dream. In the whole of our body the forces of digestion and growth are guided and given form out of dreaming.

A dream repeated at intervals over the years shows that when the central core of being has completed bodily transformation into a new capacity, the forces at work briefly rise into consciousness, enabling us to be aware of and work on the newly won faculty. The whole being of mankind is involved in continuous self-transformation – the hidden depths of the soul contain much greater wisdom than we realise.

26. In Relation to the Outside World

What we perceive with the senses as firmly outlined must be given a soft and plastic form capable of living in the etheric body, in such a way that the ego and astral body can separate from it during sleep. The astral body takes up an experience at once, the etheric needs longer. So we have to sleep on a daytime experience, reforming and reshaping it, enabling it to be transformed into a memory and united with the experiences of the etheric body. Two and a half to three days are needed in order to imprint what we experience in our soul upon the etheric, though sometimes only one and a half, but never without having slept on it. These interacting currents bring about a common resultant between the life of the individual and cosmic life. The dream is actually an outward expression of this struggle on the verge of sleeping and waking.

In most dreams we behold our etheric body, in which all our memories from the whole of our present life are simultaneously present, even those which have sunk deeply into the depths of the soul. What fills our perception when we dream is the etheric substance permeating the world with its inner processes, and all that lives in it. But we can only perceive a part of it, mainly our own etheric body and its incredibly complex processes. The dream is thus a piece of the etheric world grasped with our etheric antennae and set down in another place; and some part of these elaborate processes in the etheric body comes to awareness where the veil has been lifted. However, we don't perceive within the etheric world that surrounds us, because the force of our soul is not strong enough.[84]

In disorderly dreams it is primarily the etheric body that is active and in contact with the external world; in symbolic dramatic dreams it is the astral body that transforms the outer world into symbols and metaphors. Moreover, at each moment when awake we have an immense number of sense-impressions of which we are not aware, and dreams are so hard to understand because they contain those pictures of which we were not conscious.

If you were to notice more carefully certain dreams that are quite inexplicable you would find that these are things which might have happened, and have only been prevented because hindrances have come in the way. Our etheric body connects us also to experiences distant in time, but we only dream of something that happened many years ago if something has recently occurred related to it by some thought or feeling. If what lives in the soul is strong enough this too can force itself into our dream. The key lies in studying the dream's dramatic course and the effect it has on the dreamer's soul and spirit.

Dreams should not only be related to our inner life – certain aspects of the whole world are woven into them. Nature dreams in seed and embryo, its very essence is the weaving life of a dream; that is why we cannot enter it with the intellect.[85] Indeed the dream protests against the laws of nature. Just as gravity diminishes with the square of the distance, so too the truth of natural law diminishes, and instead the law of dreams begins to hold sway.

Intuition shows that dreaming also underlies the concepts of social, moral and political life. This is the secret of such life, which cannot be reached by thinking. The impulses that live in history, driving it forwards, live not in waking consciousness but in dreams; ordinary consciousness can only apprehend the concepts of history in dream-consciousness. They can be grasped solely through Imagination and Inspiration. The Christ impulse has worked through the centuries in the subconscious forces of the soul – indicated to us for example in the dreams of Constantine in the fourth century and of the Maid of Orleans in the fifteenth; both brought about significant historical changes.

For prosaic existence we have to thank the power of dreaming that we have a memory, for the same forces are at work in both. Dreams consisting of memories of, for example, a life of drudgery are unhealthy, they make us wake up tired; whereas fantastic dreams, such as those of flying (which generally arise from an abnormality in the lungs), work in a healthy way and we wake up bright and breezy.

27. In Relation to the Spiritual World

The world of dream pictures is like a veil concealing the spiritual world. Though unprepared we sink into the reality of the soul world and spiritland. Generally speaking, people get to the boundary, then something strange happens. The soul sees itself with all its weaknesses and failings, but cannot tolerate it. Through the horror it feels it deadens its consciousness, enabling Luciferic impulses to assert themselves, Lucifer unites with

Ahriman, and entrance to the spiritual world is barred. But if we pass the Guardian of the Threshold without knowing it, what meets us is whirling confusion.

Experiences in three different worlds – physical world, soul world, world of spirit – are chaotically combined according to inappropriate physical laws, which is why our dream world is so completely disorganised. Since, however, the ego's influence on the dreaming astral body is unconscious, nothing deriving from dream life can be a direct source of spiritual-scientific knowledge of higher worlds.

Only when our ideas and feelings go beyond daily life can our dreams have an origin in the spirit. The dream, which is a kind of wonder, cannot be reached through natural scientific measures. Whereas an untrained person experiences the astral world chaotically in dreams, the trained clairvoyant sees that world in regular forms. At first there will be transient realities surging up and down, but occurring in a regular way. The spiritual researcher, however, learns in Imagination how their symbols are formed according to the laws of the spiritual world. That ordinary consciousness perceives this world as fantastic is due to our inability to understand it – we ourselves introduce the fanciful. Our dreams can become even more peculiar if our days are not well-ordered. There is a continual interplay between that which seeks to dissolve into dreamlike fantasy and delude the dreamer, and that which represents the truth of the spiritual world.

In sleep we are cut off both from the environment and from our bodies. Impressions may come, but the soul replaces them by symbols e.g. the sound of a clock's pendulum can become the tramping of horses – just as anyone who rises to the spiritual world has to express their experiences in symbols. (That is why the first stage is called Imaginative cognition). What dreams within our soul is our spiritual eternal core. Dreams are not just a matter of symbols, as psychoanalysts think – what counts is the inner dramatic movement. The dream points the way into the subconscious and unconscious foundations of the soul; but what it brings forth is only a disguise for what is actually being experienced in the dream.

Within the dream itself, as it weaves its way before us, we have no clear awareness of self. We need to be aware that we ourselves are the governing power of our dreams. Dreams portray all kinds of things that we do not confess in waking life, or on which we do not trust ourselves to give final judgment. They reveal what we carry while awake as subconscious images, and form themselves without our will, bringing inexplicable moods of cheerfulness or depression.

There are also dreams in which we confront ourselves objectively as an ego, but do not recognise ourselves. That is a piece of self-perception outside the physical body. It is as if the ego split into two, and one ego observed the other. Such dreams depend not on the etheric body but on a piece of our astral body revealing itself outside the body. However, in dreams we perceive only the part of ourselves that has separated, not the subjective ego. Most people cannot remember that in the actual dream the subjective ego was extinguished.

When in a dream we are occupied with a problem, someone may appear who solves the problem or advises us what to do, someone who is better, cleverer than we are. This too is a doubling of the ego. We should pay attention to such dreams. In the examination dream (one who knows and one who does not) something is woven which throughout life pulsates in the depths of the soul and is connected with an inward struggle, inner soul forces not outwardly apparent – we would be too distracted if we always had it before our spiritual eyes.

If our whole I were involved, we should participate in life to the same extent that we actively participate in dreams. Powerful people would change their lives as much as they change their dreams, whilst the weaker would scarcely alter them. But only a part arises from human nature, the rest is done for us by spiritual beings.[86] The course of the dream, how we take hold of and link the pictures, their configuration, shows the way we act in life.

In any dream, what is lived through in the spiritual world during sleep is reflected down at the moment of waking, and then by means of the etheric body is reflected before the soul in the form of dream-images. These images are transformations of the spiritual truth due to its working on the physical and etheric bodies. The dreams may depend on how we regard the body when we return to it – as a house with one door, as a coffin and a corpse, or as an angel who extends to us a chalice.

Even as we half consciously witness in dreams the creative forces through which we are woven out of the cosmos, the astral, kindling us to life, becomes visible as it flows into the etheric body. In the lighting up of dreams, creative thoughts are still alive. (It is only after we waken that thought is gathered up into the forces whereby it dies and becomes a shadow.)

We may feel that something is urging us to think quite differently about certain things and then have a very striking dream. Here it is not the form but the content of the dream that is important. Suppose a man dreamt that some unknown person he cannot even think of comes to him and various things happen. Finally he realises that someone who died fifteen years ago is working into his night consciousness. Raphael was influenced by his father in this way. *Such experiences will become increasingly familiar. Thus will spirituality again be instilled into culture.*[87]

We can even dream in sense-pictures of a higher super-sensible world – artists and poets have to transpose such dreams into imaginative fantasies of waking life. In art we create from within something like that which the dream world creates from without. We have to thank the power of dreaming that there is art, for the way we feel or create beauty is very similar to the weaving creative process of dreaming.

The increasing and decreasing intensity in dreams on waking, though chaotic, belongs when ordered to the realm of music, whose plastic 'time shapes' are experienced in sleep, though unconsciously. In such dreams we can catch in their inner movements an echo of the planetary movements.

By far the majority of our dreams are spun from echoes of the sense of hearing, for between the senses of hearing and thought lies an inner sense which is quite stunted in modern life. When one has lived one's way into the spiritual world it becomes active. It resounds best when one tries to develop the after-taste of music and poetry; when one can hear the inaudible it becomes conscious.[88]

Daydreams, which are always present beneath the thoughts that we control, differ from ordinary dreams only in being less vivid, more like mental pictures. All kinds of memories may arise, and link up (just as in dreams) with other thoughts, perhaps based merely on a similarity of sounds. They fructify us artistically. A dream or hallucination with its strange images is an important cosmic riddle, illogical and amoral, but a clear hint of a spiritual world.

The Angelic world, where wakeful artistic imagination has its roots, also comes to expression in dreams. It can become pure fantasy if a Luciferic element enters; or our dreams may degenerate into all kinds of strange things that we may take for real, if influenced by Ahrimanic elements. Yet when dreams are 'innocent' and purely human, the Angel lives in them. We are nearest to the Angel when dreams arise that have something to do with our individual being, dreams which on the one hand deny, yet on the other hold fast to our consciousness adapted to the mineral world. Were our mineral consciousness not coloured by moral experience that reaches up to dreams, we could not have even a sub-conscious relationship to the Angel.

Anyone who in full consciousness experiences his dreams on falling asleep is well acquainted with the gnomes; symbolic sense-pictures of inner organs (the heart as stove, the lungs as wings) are masks for a host of goblins. If perceived unprepared these gnomes would be symbols of death, destructive forces; we should feel entombed by them. In deep sleep the undines become visible to Inspiration as a world of ever-changing beings, continually rising and sinking again like the waves of the sea. Were the waking dreams unmasked, we should be confronted by sylphs as an actual inflowing of light, either attacking or caressing. The fire-beings make waking thoughts perceptible.[89] If we enter dream-life with undeveloped judgment, all kinds of elemental beings appear and create delusions; there is always a protest against the natural order – this is the first step into the spiritual world.

Dreams which remain unconscious in the soul's depths may be perceived spiritually, and that is how fairy tale images and invisible playmates arise. The remote past of evolution too lies behind a veil of dreams, revealing our connection with divine spiritual Beings. To understand Orion we should begin to dream, like the shepherds of old. This is the realm the Greeks called 'chaos'. In modern times ordinary sleep is crumbling to pieces, and dreams will become dulled, overlaid by our abstract thinking.

28. Dreams and Destiny

The essential thing is the dream's dramatic course, which often has its source in past lives, or may point to future incarnations. It is the unwinding thread of destiny, our individual core, which plays into dreams. We are outside the body with the ego that we take from one incarnation to another and we are in our astral body, which means that we live within all the processes and beings that surround us before and after earthly life.

When we are awake our head dreams continually, drawing from the deeds of our last life, though the interpretation of this underlying dream life is difficult. During the night, the metabolic-limb man, with the sexual organization where everything is as yet undifferentiated, points forward to future earth lives (this runs parallel to the dull sleep consciousness). The chest man dreams of the previous and following periods between death and rebirth, interweaving the two sets of forces in outbreathing and inbreathing respectively – more dull by day, brighter during sleep. This we may perceive as our feelings.[90]

When we become more careful in analysing dream life – and every aspiring esotericist should do so – we shall gradually notice things we could not have experienced in this incarnation.

Human beings today feel the urge to investigate dreams because they feel instinctively that their thoughts and perceptions do not give them anything for their soul life. Souls feel within themselves not only impulses from past lives, but also an echo of life before birth. This is the case for most of us.

Spiritually the dream is the person, as the seed is the plant. Foreign to the present life, the dream is the seed of the next life, and we learn to feel it within the withering organs from the past life. To Imagination the metabolic-limb system appears to be withering least of all, and most connected as to form and content with the person's future. When we try to understand the latter, the intellect is of no help; we have to dream of the human being while awake.[91]

We may dream of doing something with a friend twenty years ago, yet it may point to the next incarnation, for the etheric body has only past images to work with. We really have prophecies in us, and it is most important to attend to them. All dreams are in fact prophetic; when we dream we always dream the future. Thus in dreams is revealed what is related to the future, but only to what is great and cosmic, not to the details of life. But because we cannot formulate mental pictures of future events, we clothe the dream in pictures of past ones, and draw them like a veil over the inner experience. However, one misunderstands the dream regarding it only as a prophecy. When someone is in a dreamy state during waking life, it is not without effect on his karma.

We belong in dreams to the cosmos as a whole, the clear-cut forms of daily life melting away like salt dissolved in a liquid. We find ourself within the being who goes through repeated earth lives in a realm opposed to nature's laws; it seems as if what we normally see in sharp outlines when awake were born out of the fluid and volatile. Set free from nature, the ego can prepare itself in Imaginations, which are strong impulses for what it will do after death. Dreams show this in illusory form, they are like a window behind which the ego weaves from one life to the next.[92]

Dreams are nearly always a companionship with the dead around us, but usually due to our own need to come near to them. When one knows one is not asleep in the ordinary way, but consciousness of the spiritual world awakens during actual sleep, then our activity is most closely related to that of the dead, who are living through their nights from their time on earth.

Anyone wishing to consider dreams relating to the deceased will need to consult the lecture *The Dead Are With Us*,[93] where all aspects, including the dangers, are described. It is essential to know that the dead speak from within us, whereas our own thoughts confront us.

29. Transforming Dream Life

With every new stage of evolution an element from the past which has atrophied reappears as ferment for subsequent development, like yeast that makes the dough rise. The whole purpose of earlier times was to allow us to enter spiritual worlds during sleep, whereas today we have to prepare to enter whilst awake.

Since the middle of the 15th century we have had little inclination simply to experience the images of dreams, only to interpret them. But today we begin to sleep differently, and dream life must not be interpreted intellectually. We are starting to take images out of sleep which want to live not in our ego alone, where reason rules, but also in our astral body. If we work against this we are working against the whole course of evolution. Our culture must be filled as much as we can with what is connected with the spiritual world; we have to bring what is experienced in sleep into waking life in such a way that our astral body, not our ego, becomes permeated with images. Today people receive little in the way of Imaginations out of their sleep life, and we have to make alive again the images that lived within us before birth in an endeavour to reach a deeper life of the spirit.[94]

Our present dreaming will beget a new kind of vision, a perception of the astral and spiritual worlds, as is already the case with initiates. The astral body can only have its higher sense organs developed when they are carved into it during sleep, while outside the body. Indirectly this is possible when impressions made by day upon the physical body remain within the astral body when it withdraws. Only through meditation and concentration exercises acting intensely upon the astral body can the new organs be plastically reshaped and developed during sleep.[95]

One who has followed energetically the indications in *Knowledge of Higher Worlds* for a long time, even perhaps for several decades, will notice his dreams gradually begin to change. As if awakening from a dream, a kind of memory may arise. The whole mood of soul brings a wonderful elation to realise that in the depths something more is active than in ordinary consciousness. Through strong effort we have the power to plunge into a new world. But for this to occur we must be able to exclude the recollections and images of ordinary life which concerned our particular selves in the outer world. Reality only begins on that higher level.

Dreams are normally connected with our own organism, but when we connect with our surroundings and at the same time develop the forces that we develop in dreams, we experience Imaginative thinking. We can then experience consciously elemental forms of nature where life is interrupted and does not attain its goal.[96]

In Imagination we do not simply remember what is dreamt, but look at it and reach a true concept of what a dream is, interpreting it rightly in relation to the spiritual (mostly moral) world. We should not only look at the symbolical course, but question ourselves morally about it. The symbolical pictures bring out our true nature, spiritual beings speak through them, and we can gain self-knowledge from them. Pursuit by wild beasts may, for example, indicate animal instincts behind our self-justification.

Dreams lift out of the depths of soul something that we cannot lift by memory, but is within reach of the subconscious, half-conscious dream state. The seeker then always finds himself in true self-knowledge, as in Imagination, but that may present itself objectively, as if it were the external world. A systematic higher development of dream consciousness is all that is required to come to the first stage of supersensible consciousness. If deep sleep consciousness awakens outside the body, it is the second supersensible stage of consciousness.

Thus dreams, until now confused and haphazard, begin to assume a more regular character; images revealing law, cause and effect, succeed each other in sensible connections like the ideas of daily life. Pictures appear of a world hitherto unknown, though symbolical presentation remains unchanged. Very soon they may be intellectually mastered and controlled, and the dreamer is aware of this. With spiritual knowledge we can say what in reality is then dreaming, namely the eternal spiritual core of the human being. This is not yet, however, any basis for an authoritative account of the higher worlds, which can only gradually be attained.*

By means of thought that stimulates itself over and over again from one's inner self, one can bring the work of the soul into the full light of consciousness. Thus one comes to compelling the dream to manifest itself in the light of consciousness, it is held fast as if in a strong container. In its spiritual vision of itself, the soul so grows in strength that it perceives its own higher reality, of which it recognises the body to be the imitation.

* See further *Knowledge of the Higher Worlds*, chapters on 'Transformation of Dream Life' and 'Continuity of Consciousness', or *Occult Science* (5).

REFERENCES

Except where specified, all references are from the work of Rudolf Steiner and published by either Rudolf Steiner Press (rudolfsteinerpress.org), Steiner Books (steinerbooks.org) or Mercury Press. They may be borrowed from libraries of the Anthroposophical Society in many countries.
GA refers to Gesamtausgabe = collected works of Rudolf Steiner in German.

PREFACE
1. 6.11.16 *Karma of (Human) Vocation* (3) GA1/2
    22.10.15 *The Occult Movement in the 19th Century* (7) GA254
    24.8.13 *Secrets of the Threshold* (1) GA147

I INTRODUCTION
2. 2.9.23 *The Healing Process* (1) GA319
3. 19.5.08 *Gospel of St. John* (2) GA103
4. 22.6.24 *Karmic Relationships Volume II* (26) GA 236
5. 20.5.08 *Gospel of St. John* (3) GA103
6. 21.8.23 *Evolution of the World and of Humanity / Evolution of Consciousness* (3), *Sleep and Dreams* (extr.) (9) GA227
7. 9.10 18 *What does the Angel do in Our Astral Body / The Work of the Angels in Man's Astral Body / Angels* GA182

II GOING TO SLEEP
8. 9.10.22 *Sleep and Dreams* (4) GA218
9. 2.1.22 *Soul Economy and Waldorf Education* (11) GA303
10. 4.9.19 *Study of Man* (13) / *Foundations of Human Experience* GA293
11. 22.3.20 *Introducing Anthroposophical Medicine / Spiritual Science and Medicine* (2) GA312
12. 21.3.12 *Anthroposophical Quarterly 17:2*: The Nature of Eternity GA61

13. 16.1.21   Typescript R81: Relationship of the Diverse Branches of
              Natural Science to Astronomy (16) GA323
14. 12.11.21 *Cosmosophy Volume II* (10) GA208
15. 9.5.14   *How the Spiritual World interpenetrates the Physical* GA261
16. 23.4.24   *Course for Young Doctors* (3) GA316
17. 16.6.10   *Mission of the Individual Folk Souls* (10) GA121
18. 21.12.12 Untranslated GA62
19. 7.4.20   *Health Care as a Social Issue* GA314
20. 29.8.24   *The Healing Process* (2) GA319
21.   *Fundamental Principes of Curative Eurythmy.* Floris Books.
              M. Kirchner-Bockholt. ISBN 9780854403219
22.   *A Guide to Child Health.* Floris Books. ISBN 9780863153907
23. 21.5.10   *Manifestations of Karma* (6) GA120
24. 19.1.22   *Old and New Methods of Initiation* (4) GA210

III FIRST PHASE OF SLEEP

25. 10.12.12 *Between Death and Rebirth* (4) (*Life between...*) GA141
26. 25.11.23 *Mystery Centres / Mystery Knowledge and Mystery Centres* (3)
              GA232
27. 6.3.17   *Cosmic and Human Metamorphoses* (5) GA175
28. 28.8.20   *Spiritual Science as a Foundation for Social Forms* (10) GA199
29. 3.12.22   *Man and the World of Stars and the Spiritual Communion of
              Mankind* (3) / *Sleep and Dreams* (3) GA219
30. 19.1.22   *Old and New Methods of Initiation* (4) GA210
31. 5.11.22   *Concealed Aspects of Human Existence* GA218
    27.8.23   *Evolution of Consciousness / Evolution of the World and of
              Humanity* (9) GA227
32. 30.9.21   *Cosmosophy Volume I* (3) GA207
    8.7.21   *Man in the Cosmos as a Being of Thought and Will / Sleep and
              Dreams* (6) GA205
33. 3.2.23   *Earthly Knowledge and Heavenly Wisdom* (1) GA221
34. 3.2.24   *Anthroposophy : an Introduction / Anthroposophy and the
              Inner Life* (6) GA234
35. 2.5.23   *Golden Blade 1951 / Anthroposophical Review 6:2*: Cosmic
              Word and Individual Man GA224
    14.9.24   *Pastoral Medicine* (7) / *Broken Vessels* GA318

36. 25.3.13   *Effects of Occult Development / Spiritual Development / Esoteric
             Development* (6) GA145
37.ʰ 3.3.10   *Metamorphoses of the Soul Volume II* (5) GA59
38. 19.5.23   *Man's Being, his Destiny and World Evolution* (4) GA226
39. 1.10.21   *Cosmosophy Volume I* (4) GA207

IV SECOND PHASE OF SLEEP

40. 21.8.23   *Evolution of Consciousness / Evolution of the World and of
             Humanity* (3) / *Sleep and Dreams* (9) GA227
41. 2.5.23   *Golden Blade 1951 / Anthroposophical Review 6:2*: Cosmic
             Word and Individual Man GA224
42. 21.12.08 *The Being of Man and his Future Evolution* (4) GA107
43. 6.5.22   *Human Soul in Relation to World Evolution* (4) GA212
44. 27.8.23   *Evolution of Consciousness / Evolution of the World and of
             Humanity* (9) GA227
45. 20.5.13   *Michaelmas / Festivals and their Meaning* GA152
46. 17.7.21   *Guardian Angels* GA205
47. 21.8.10   *Genesis / Biblical Secrets of Creation* (6) GA122

V THIRD PHASE OF SLEEP

48. 28.8.20   *Spiritual Science as a Foundation for Social Forms* (10) GA199
49. 17.4.20   *Man: Hieroglyph of the Universe / Mystery of the Universe* (5)
             GA201
50. 2.5.23   *Golden Blade 1951 / Anthroposophical Review 6:2*: Cosmic
             Word and Individual Man GA224
51. 9.10.22   *Anthroposophical Quarterly 10:3* Experiences of Sleep / *Sleep
             and Dreams* (4) GA218
52. 21.3.13   *Effects of Occult Development / Spiritual Development / Esoteric
             Development* (2) GA145
53. 3.12.22   *Man and the World of the Stars and the Spiritual Communion
             of Mankind* (3), *Sleep and Dreams* (3) GA219
54. 6.3.17   *Cosmic and Human Metamorphoses* (5) GA175
55. 25.3.13   *Effects of Occult Development / Spiritual Development / Esoteric
             Development* (6) GA145
56. 25.9.17   *Karma of Materialism* (9) GA176
57. 26.6.21   *Therapeutic Insights* (2) GA205
58. 12.11.21 *Cosmosophy Volume II* (10) GA208

59. 12.11.22 *Planetary Spheres and their influence on Man's Life on Earth and in Spiritual Worlds* (1) GA218
60. 4.6.08 *Influence of Spiritual Beings on Man* (10)/ *Nature Spirits* GA102
61. 12.11.21 *Cosmosophy Volume II* (10) GA208
62. 14.1.17 *Karma of Untruthfulness Volume II* (19) GA174
63. 22.6.24 *Karmic Relationships Volume II* (15) GA236
    14.6.24 *Karmic Relationships Volume VII* (8) GA239
64. 24.3.22 *Anthroposophy Today 4*: The Three Stages of Sleep GA211
65. 30.9.21 *Cosmosophy Volume I* (3) GA207

VI REVERSION TO FIRST PHASE
66. Principal Sources Only
    24.11.10 *Sleep and Dreams* (1) GA60
    10.12.12 *Between Death and Rebirth* (4) (*Life between...*) GA141
    3.9.10 *Gospel of St. Matthew* (3) GA123
    13.11.21 *Cosmosophy Volume II* (11) GA208
    1.10.11 *Etherisation of the Blood / Reappearance of Christ in the Etheric / Esoteric Christianity* GA130
    5.12.12 Untranslated GA62

VII WAKING UP
67. 22.12.22 *Man and the World of Stars and the Spiritual Communion of Mankind* (7) GA219
68. 30.9.21 *Cosmosophy Volume I* (3) GA207
69. 9.7.21 Typescript Z 325: Man in the Cosmos as a Being of Thought and Will (2) GA205
70. 29.12.22 *Man and the World of Stars and the Spiritual Communion of Mankind* (10) / *Reverse Ritual* GA219
71. 27.8.19 *Study of Man* (6) / *Foundations of Human Experience* (6) GA293
72. 27.6.24 *Curative Education / Education for Special Needs* (3) GA317
73. 7.1.21 Typescript R81: Relationship of the Diverse Branches of Natural Science to Astronomy (7) GA323
74. 22.6.24 *Karmic Relationships Volume II* (15) or (26) GA236
    14.6.24 *Karmic Relationships Volume VII* (8) GA239
75. 10.12.12 *Between Death and Rebirth* (4) (*Life between...*) GA141
76. 14.6.24 *Karmic Relationships Volume VII* (8) GA239

77. 16.10 15 *Occult Movement in the 19th Century* (3) GA254
78. 23.3.10 *Macrocosm and Microcosm* (3) / *Sleep and Dreams* (3) GA119
79. 12.6.19 *Some Characteristics of Today* / *The Meaning of Life* GA193
    13.9.19 *Problems of Our Time* (2) / *Guardian Angels* GA193
80.   *Verses and Meditations.* tr. George Adams
            Truth-Wrought-Words. tr. Arvia MacKaye Ege
            Breathing the Spirit. tr. Matthew Barton

VIII DREAMS

81. 14.4.23 Typescript Z171: Of Thought, Feeling and Will in Their
            Relation to Sleep GA84
82. 29.5.15 (NSL145) *Anthroposophic News Sheet* 3:36-37: Characteristics
            of Man's Occult Development GA162
83. 16.9.22 *Human Being in Body, Soul and Spirit* (6) / *From Crystals to
            Crocodiles* (6) / *Nutrition* GA347
84. 18.4.14 *Presence of the Dead on the Spiritual Path* / *Sleep and Dreams*
            (8) GA154
85. 24.8.23 *Evolution of Consciousness* / *Evolution of the World and of
            Humanity* (6) GA227
86. 8.2.24 *Anthroposophy: an Introduction* (7) / *Anthroposophy and the
            Inner Life* (7) / *Sleep and Dreams* (13) GA234
87. 20.5.12 *Earthly and Cosmic Man* (7) GA133
88. 13.4.13 Untranslated GA150
89. 3.11.23 *Man as Symphony of the Creative Word* / *Harmony of the
            Creative Word* (8) / *Nature Spirits* GA230
90. 25.6.18 Typescript C50: A Sound Outlook for Today (1) GA181
91. 9.2.24 *Anthroposophy: an Introduction* (8) / *Anthroposophy and the
            Inner Life* (8) / *Sleep and Dreams* (14) GA234
92. 22.8.23 *Evolution of Consciousness* / *Evolution of the World and of
            Humanity* (4) / *Sleep and Dreams* (10) GA227
93. 10.2.18 *The Dead are with us* / *Life beyond Death* / *Staying Connected*
            (8) / *Death as Metamorphosis of Life* GA183
94. 11.9.20 *Spiritual Science as a Foundation for Social Forms* (16) / *Sleep
            and Dreams* (12) GA199
95. 30.5.08 *Gospel of St. John* (11) GA103
96. 16.12.17 *Influence of the Dead on Destiny* (6) GA179